# WELLS CATHEDRAL

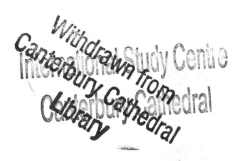

*The New Bell's Cathedral Guides*
# WELLS CATHEDRAL

L. S. COLCHESTER

PHOTOGRAPHY BY GEORGE H. HALL

## UNWIN HYMAN
LONDON   SYDNEY

*For*
*The Friends of*
*Wells Cathedral*

First published in Great Britain by Unwin
Hyman, an imprint of Unwin Hyman Limited,
1987

UNWIN HYMAN LIMITED
Denmark House, 37–39 Queen Elizabeth Street,
London SE1 2QB

and

40 Museum Street, London WC1A 1LU

Allen & Unwin Australia Pty Ltd
8 Napier Street, North Sydney, NSW 2060,
Australia

Allen & Unwin New Zealand Ltd with the Port Nicholson Press
60 Cambridge Terrace, Wellington, New Zealand

ISBN 0–04–440015–2
ISBN 0–04–440012–8 Pbk

*British Library Cataloguing in Publication Data*

Colchester, L. S.
Wells Cathedral.—(The New Bell's cathedral
guides)
1. Wells Cathedral—Guide-books
I. Title
942.3'83   DA690.W46

Designed by Colin Lewis
Printed in Great Britain at the University Press,
Cambridge

# CONTENTS

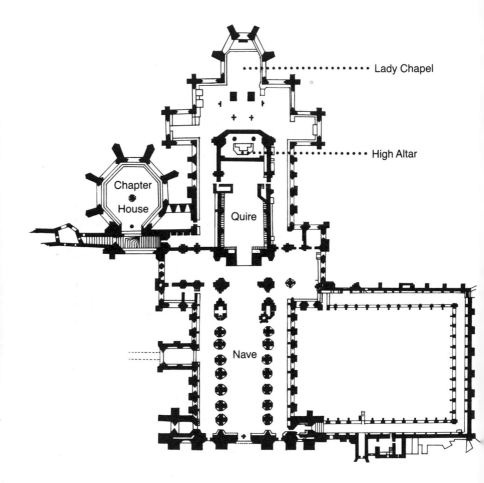

Lady Chapel

High Altar

Chapter House

Quire

Nave

*Plan of Wells Cathedral.*

*Chapter One*

# OUTLINE HISTORY OF THE CATHEDRAL

Roughly in line with the front row of chairs in the cathedral nave is a modern stone with the inscription INA REX 688–726. This is a replacement, put there by Dean Armitage Robinson, of a much earlier stone in honour of Ine, King of Wessex, whom tradition has named as the founder of the church of Wells, *c.*705. The tradition may be true, but records of Ine's life and actions surviving outside Wells make no mention of it. It is a purely local tradition of which there is no firm proof or disproof. What is certain is that Aldhelm, Bishop of Sherborne, founded a church here *c.*705, but whether under the direction and patronage of the king, we do not know.

By 766 Cynewulf, King of Wessex, endowed 'the minster beside the great spring called Wielea [Wells] with two hides of land for the benefit of the minster, and that the priests there may the more diligently serve only God in the church of St Andrew the Apostle'. So already the dedication of the church to the first of the apostles is made clear. The church was given cathedral status *c.*909.

Knowledge of the Saxon church at this time is based almost entirely on the excavations undertaken east of the cloisters between 1978 and 1980, which not only confirmed, but considerably added to, the information gained from a previous excavation in 1894. Dr Warwick Rodwell not only found successive chapels enlarged and extended, but also what appeared to be the foundations of a Roman mausoleum. Previously it had been thought that the Romans, although they undoubtedly mined lead on the Mendips, and left roads going to and from their mining areas, as well as a small amphitheatre at Charterhouse-on-Mendip, had completely by-passed or ignored the site of the present city. The early Christian chapels were aligned on St Andrew's well, which seems to have been regarded as a holy well. A small aperture in the present fourteenth-century wall looks straight on to this well, which is the small spring in the part of the bishop's garden known as 'Scotland'. (This is not to be confused with the main group of three wells named 'St Andrew's Well' incorrectly on the Ordnance Survey map.)

Just visible at the extreme west of the excavations, almost wholly covered by the east cloister walk, was the curve of the main apse, proving St John Hope's theory of 1909 that the old cathedral building lay, roughly parallel to the present path, across the site of the present cloister garth ('Palm Church-yard'). After St John Hope's paper was read in 1909 one canon observed that it was 'very interesting speculation. But because it was interesting, they must not forget that it was also speculation.' Since then people have accepted Hope's speculation as almost entirely correct; and it is most gratifying now to have proof of it.

The nave, probably without aisles, extended towards the market-place. So when in the mid-twelfth century Bishop Robert permitted the holding of fairs in the market-place on three days of the year, he stipulated that their stalls must not encroach upon the forecourt of the cathedral. He was referring, of course, to the old West Front, not the present one.

Giso of Lorraine became bishop in 1060, when Edward the Confessor was king of England. Giso's short autobiography has come down to us and is available in print. While Edward was generous to the church, Duke Harold, his nephew, was depriving the see of some of its property, so much so that the bishop considered excommunicating him. On the death of the Confessor, Giso again appealed to Harold to restore what he had taken. Harold promised to do so, but before he did anything about it, William of Normandy had landed and defeated Harold at Hastings on 14 October 1066. Within a year the Conqueror restored to Giso all that Harold had taken.

This had an interesting sequel at Wells. 14 October, the date of William's victory at Hastings, is the Saint's Day of a fairly obscure third-century Pope, Calixtus I, who was murdered. Wells had a chapel dedicated to St Calixtus; his day was one of the three days on which fairs were permitted by Bishop Robert: Invention of Holy Cross (3 May), St Calixtus (14 October) and St Andrew's Day (30 November). To this list Bishop Reginald added the anniversary of the dedication of the chapel of St Thomas the Martyr (i.e. Becket) in Southover, Wells (25 June). And King John in his Charter of 7 September 1201 added a fifth fair, to be held on the Feast of the Translation of St Andrew (9 May).

So the townspeople, whose sympathies at that stage no doubt lay with Harold, a good Anglo-Saxon, rather than the foreigner, William, could rejoice over the martyrdom of St Calixtus, while the bishop and his following could celebrate the victory of the generous Conqueror and the downfall of the selfish, thieving Harold.

St Calixtus's Day was further enhanced in mediaeval Wells, because that is the day on which the relics of saints, kept under lock and key in the cathedral, were displayed annually and carried in procession.

It may be of interest to note that until the outbreak of the Second World War fairs came to Wells and filled the market-place with their stalls, dodgems, big wheels and merry-go-rounds on four of these days. They came at the weekend nearest to 3 May (some people thought they were celebrating May Day), went away and returned for the following week-end (approximately 9 May); returned in October and again in November, for St Calixtus and St Andrew. Now they come only twice: at the beginning of May and again in early November, on the day of the Wells Carnival, which falls halfway between St Calixtus and St Andrew.

Worse was to befall on the death of Giso, a year after the death of William I. For Giso of Lorraine was succeeded by John of Tours, also called John de Villula, who had no love or regard for Wells at all. He destroyed the dormitory, refectory and cloister at Wells where the canons, although they were never monks, lived together as a community after the Lotharingian pattern. Some of the building materials were re-used to build the bishop a country house, and rents belonging to the church were handed over to the bishop's brother, Hildebert, whom he appointed provost, and to his heirs.

Meanwhile John transferred the see to Bath, where he dismissed all the monks as being an ignorant lot, and imported

9

some new and more intelligent monks from overseas. Hildebert's son was Archdeacon of Wells, who inherited the rents and provostship from his father, and passed them on to his brother and heir, Reginald (not to be confused with the later bishop), who was precentor.

Most commentators on the whole exercise of the transference of the see from Wells to Bath associate it with the resolution of the Council of London in 1075. This named the transference of the sees of Sherborne to Sarum, Lichfield to Chester and Selsey to Chichester, but did not include Wells. Only Polydore Virgil writing in 1534 mentions a later Council of London in 1078 which named the new intended sees of Bath, Lincoln and Exeter (although the see had already been moved from Crediton to Exeter in 1050). Being entirely the bishop's manor, Wells did not get much of a write-up in Domesday Book, but its population cannot have been very far short of Bath's at that time, especially as Bath had recently been sacked and burnt after the Domesday count, only shortly before the transfer there of the see. In 250 years' time the population of Wells was to exceed that of Bath quite considerably. John of Tours, the bishop, was a practising physician, we know: it may have been the curative powers of the Bath waters which induced him to transfer the see to a town with a much longer history, and a borough, a compact town within its own walls, while Wells was still very much the sort of sprawling rural area we now know as 'St Cuthbert Out' parish. Finally, Bath was considerably nearer to Worcester, then culturally supreme.

Robert of Lewes, bishop from 1136 to 1166, rebuilt the abbey church at Bath and also tried to raise the status of Wells once again. He is said to have rebuilt the cathedral here, which was consecrated and dedicated jointly by him and the bishops of Salisbury, Worcester and Hereford in 1148. But it is unthinkable that a new cathedral should be replaced and swept away little more than thirty years later. Surely what happened was that the Wells church was thoroughly restored after being neglected, and aisles probably built along the long nave, so that proper processions could be held on every Feast day. Now was the time the full cathedral worship could be held in Wells, and that is why four bishops took part in the consecration. Robert re-organized the Wells Chapter and drew up statutes, which ultimately appeared as what are now known as the *Statuta Antiqua*, from which it is clear that Wells already had its full complement of dignitaries, canons, prebendaries (22, in addition to the deanery, gradually increased to 55), vicars choral and choristers, and a Choristers' School as well as a Grammar School for clerks in training.

After Robert's death in 1166 there was a long interregnum. This was the period of Henry II's quarrel with Becket, which culminated in Becket's murder on 29 December 1170. As part of the king's expiation he was ordered by the Pope to fill all vacant sees without delay. Reginald de Bohun, Archdeacon of Salisbury, and son of Jocelyn, then Bishop of Salisbury, was chosen as Bishop of Bath. He had been a friend of Becket, but had changed his allegiance when his father was excommunicated by Becket.

In 1171 Reginald was sent by the king to plead the king's innocence before the Pope. On Ash Wednesday (13 February), 1173 Becket was canonized. That same year Reginald was elected Bishop of Bath. But it was not until 23 June 1174, after being cleared of all complicity in Becket's murder, that he was consecrated bishop by Archbishop Peter of Tarentaise and Richard of Dover, the new Archbishop of Canterbury, at St Jean de Maurienne in Savoy, as Richard and he travelled back to England from Rome.

They came back via the Cotentin, apparently so that Reginald could visit his family at St Georges de Bohun, near Carentan. On his way he dedicated the new church of St Thomas the Martyr at St Lô (destroyed in the Second World War), which must have been one of the first of many churches dedicated to the recently-canonized Archbishop.

We then come upon one of those surprises (as it seems to me) on that trip. As Reginald and the Archbishop of Canterbury wait for the cross-channel boat at Barfleur, whom should they meet but the king, Henry II, going the other way. Was it pre-arranged? On arrival in England Archbishop and bishop went together straight to Canterbury, arriving there on 4 September. On 5 September the east end of Canterbury Cathedral was burnt to the ground. On 24 November 1174, while on a Visitation of the Province as Apostolic Delegate, the Archbishop enthroned the new bishop in his cathedral at Bath.

### The Present Cathedral

In 1179 or 1180 work started on the new cathedral at Wells. Reginald found the ideal master mason (or architect) for the purpose. At the coronation of Richard I in Westminster Abbey in 1189 Reginald, as one of the senior bishops, supported the king on his left side, while the Bishop of Durham took the right. At a later coronation to save confusion it was ordered that all arrangements should be as for the first coronation of Richard I, so ever since then the Bishop of Bath and Wells has had the right to apply for this position at all subsequent coronations. In 1191 Reginald was elected Archbishop of Canterbury, but died within the month.

Savaric was the next bishop. He contrived to obtain the abbacy of Glastonbury for himself and had himself designated Bishop of Bath and Glastonbury, much to the indignation of the monks there. However, he did little harm, for he absented himself from the country most of the time, and that profuse letter-writer, Peter of Blois, who was Archdeacon of Bath, wrote begging him to put in an appearance in his diocese. A Latin epigram composed after his death has been aptly translated by a Wells canon:

'Through the world travelling, all the world's guest,
His last day of life was his first day of rest.'

Jocelyn of Wells, one of the greatest of Wells's children, became bishop in 1206. He was the son of Edward of Wells, who held the estate of Wellesleigh, and a house on the corner of The Liberty, all traces of which vanished in a road-widening scheme of 1932. Jocelyn's elder brother, Hugh, was Archdeacon of Wells, and later became Bishop of Lincoln. (He must not be confused with the earlier St Hugh of Lincoln, who had been third prior and virtual re-founder of Witham Charterhouse, the earliest Carthusian house in England (situated near Frome, in Somerset).)

Hugh and Jocelyn were both friends of King John and acted as his advisers. Unfortunately, he only too frequently failed to follow their advice. The King soon quarrelled with the Pope over the choice of the new Archbishop of Canterbury, which had been referred to the Pope for settlement. The Pope's choice was Stephen Langton, then employed at the Vatican. The King refused to let him land in England. The Pope retaliated by putting England under Interdict in 1208, which meant that all churches were closed and all services suspended. It is possible to see the point in the nave where work was stopped and probably not resumed until ten or twelve years later. (See pp. 94–5.) Still Hugh and Jocelyn tried to persuade the King to give way, but without success. The Pope then

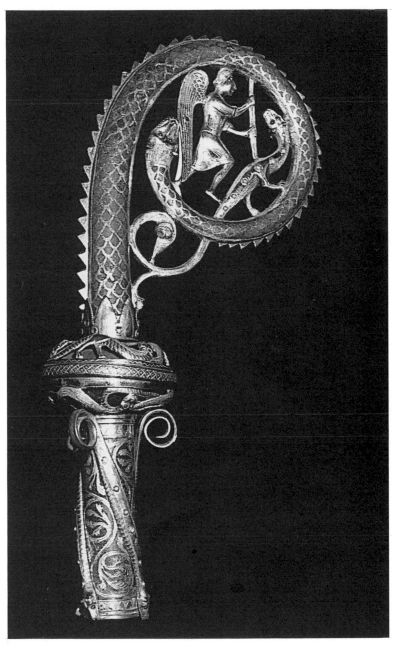

*The Limoges enamel crosier of Jocelyn, bishop 1206–42, of which 57 other similar examples are known. The diagonal arrangement of the serpents on the sleeve is unusual.*

*This head-stop at the west end of the north nave triforium, showing an old man wearing a mason's cap, is thought to depict the Master Mason, Adam Lock, who died in 1229.*

excommunicated the King. Hugh, Jocelyn and four other bishops could do no more, so in November 1209 they went into voluntary exile in France.

Hugh, already elected Bishop of Lincoln but not yet consecrated, obtained permission to be consecrated in France. The King expected him to go to the Archbishop of Rouen. Instead he was consecrated, much to the king's annoyance, by Stephen Langton, the duly appointed Archbishop of Canterbury, at Melun, on the Seine 30 miles (48 km) above Paris. The only other place we know for certain they visited during their exile, 1209–13, was St Martin-la-Garenne, a village 5 miles (8 km) from Mantes on the Seine, 40 miles (64 km) below Paris, just inside the Ile de France, not far from the border of Normandy. Until a few years before Normandy had still been part of John's domain, and Jocelyn would almost certainly have known it well from his previous visits on royal and church business. It may well have been during this period of exile that he acquired his gilt and enamelled crosier from Limoges, which has recently been dated by the experts to the first quarter of the thirteenth century. It is now preserved in the Cathedral Library display room.

King John gave in in 1213; Stephen Langton was allowed to take up his appointment in Canterbury, and the exiled bishops returned. The King failed to keep his promise to pay them all their emoluments which he had taken for himself in their absence. Consequently, at Wells, where much of the building cost was met by the bishop, work continued to be suspended, possibly until about 1220, when John's son, Henry III, granted sixty great oaks for the building of the cathedral.

In 1219 Jocelyn had surrendered his title to the Abbey of Glastonbury, which became once again independent under its own abbot, though still subject to the bishop as diocesan. Jocelyn thereby became Bishop of Bath (only). He applied to the Pope for Wells to be given full cathedral status, so that he could adopt the name and style of Bishop of Bath and Wells. The Pope wrote to the papal legate, Pandulf, Bishop of Norwich, agreeing to this, on condition that Pandulf investigated what had been done in the past, ascertaining in particular if Wells had ever been a cathedral, and whether the Somerset bishop had ever been known as Bishop of Wells (as indeed he had for 280 years). Both questions could have been answered easily in the affirmative, but Pandulf did nothing. Consequently, it was not until 1245, under Innocent IV, three Popes later, that Jocelyn's successor, Roger, was authorized and ordered to adopt the title of Bishop of Bath and Wells, as it has remained ever since.

In 1229 the Wells master mason, Adam Lock, died, bequeathing his house (on the site of the big house in The Liberty now known as The Cedars) to the Bishop's Chaplain, who made it over to the Grammar School of the Cathedral. By the time of Lock's death, the nave was probably mostly finished, and the unadorned plinth of the West Front completed. Thomas Norreys, one of the witnesses to Lock's will, who had obviously worked under him, took over as master mason and was responsible for the far more ornate character of the West Front.

At the same time as the West Front was going up Jocelyn was building his Palace, that is, the 'centre block' of the present Palace, for which Henry III provided 30 oaks in 1233.

By 1239 the West Front was high enough to link up with the nave and make it windproof and watertight. Dedication

took place on St Romanus's Day (23 October) of that year, but there was no question of its yet being finished. There was still much to be done: the gable to be completed, niches to be filled with statuary (probably filled from the bottom as work proceeded); the vault to be finished.

On 21 December 1248 there was an earth-tremor, at which a roof-boss fell from the top of the building where the workmen were still busy. As this was in the middle of winter, it must have been interior work that was going on, because outside work was not, and is not now, done because of the risk of damage by frost. On the other hand, roofs were put on as soon as the walls were high enough, so that the men could carry on with interior work 'indoors'.

Soon after the dedication, work seems to have begun on the Chapter House complex, i.e. the passage, the outside walls of the undercroft, and the staircase, which was to lead ultimately to the upstairs Chapter House. But with Jocelyn's death in 1242 and the ensuing legislation at Rome, to give the Wells Chapter the right to elect the new bishop jointly with the Chapter of Bath, all funds were dissipated (see p. 151). Work on the Chapter House was stopped for more than 40 years; the design of the centre gable of the West Front was changed and the two top rows of niches left empty, the angels and apostles not being added until the fifteenth century.

Work on the Chapter House complex was resumed in 1286 at the same time as Bishop Robert Burnell was building a new chapel at the Palace and a new banqueting hall. The Chapter House seems to have been finished by the end of 1306, since in mid-January 1307 the Chapter announced that they had spent so much on building their Chapter House that they had no money left for other expenditure.

And yet, in spite of this, the first half of the fourteenth century was a period of intense building activity at Wells, for which most of the money seems to have been raised by the Chapter. They could no longer depend on the earnings and perquisites of their bishops' high office in the royal service. But all the bishops from Drokensford onwards offered 40 days' Indulgence to subscribers to the fabric fund. Moreover, the power of the Chapter and their responsibility for the conduct and management of the cathedral was growing not only at

*OPPOSITE: The magnificent West Front, with nearly 300 mediaeval statues, begun c.1230, photographed after conservation was completed in 1986.*

*The elaborate tomb of William of March, bishop 1293–1302, with the splendidly carved figures sadly mutilated. Saint or rogue?*

Wells, but in other cathedrals too. At Wells from 1319–21 the Chapter asserted itself against the bishop, reaching a fairly hard-and-fast division of authority: while the bishop remained supreme throughout the diocese which covered the old County of Somerset, the Dean and Chapter were solely responsible for running the cathedral, and the bishop's interference was severely restricted.

By about 1320, if not before, the eastward Lady Chapel was completed, and at the same time work must have started at ground level to extend the quire eastwards to meet it. Work may have overlapped with the raising of the tower and spire. In 1200 the central tower over the crossing had risen only about 1½ feet (45 cm) above roof-level; then a temporary roof was put on (such as may still be seen at Westminster Abbey). In 1313 the tower was extended upwards (see pp. 61, 113).

There are two main reasons for thinking that the extension of the quire began as early as 1320: (a) the new stalls were ordered in 1325; (b) there are three considerable breaks in construction below window-level in the new south quire aisle, as seen from outside in the Camery (see p. 79). These may be due to inadequate foundations in land easily waterlogged; but, whatever the reason, the necessary renovation and repair must have taken considerable time. The two eastern transeptal chapels, Corpus Christi in the north, and St Katherine in the south, were finished respectively in 1328 and 1329.

These chapels, of course, were only as high as the aisles. There was still an enormous amount of work to be done to raise the quire to its full height. Money was already short, and drastic work was necessary to support the central tower.

As a means of raising funds an attempt was made in 1324 to get William of March, bishop 1293–1302, canonized. The idea seems to have originated with the then bishop, Drokensford, almost certainly as a result of the successful canonization in 1320 of Thomas Cantilupe, Bishop of Hereford 1275–1282. But though William of March may have helped the canons of Wells financially with their building scheme, he does not seem to have been a proper subject for canonization. Contemporary records relate how

'in a single day, viz: the second Sunday in July 1294, there was a survey of all church wealth throughout the kingdom, such as had never been known before or since; and one half of everything was taken to finance the Scottish wars. And this was ordered not by the king, but by the king's Treasurer, namely the bishop—nay, the tyrant—of Bath, not defending the church but taking the offensive against it.'

When the Archbishop, Robert Winchelsey, protested to the

king, Edward I disclaimed all responsibility, and blamed William of March. Besides, more than a year before these events, at the joint announcement by the Prior of Bath and the Dean of Wells in January 1293 of William of March's election as bishop, some unknown member of the public shouted out in English:

'Christescors and Seinte Marie habbe hi halle that hine chose bissop of Bathe'
(The curse of Christ and of Saint Mary on all who chose him Bishop of Bath.)

As soon as Ralph of Shrewsbury succeeded Drokensford as Bishop of Bath and Wells in 1329, all attempts to secure William's canonization were abandoned.

It was while work was proceeding on the extension to the quire that Edward III stayed in Wells from 23 December 1331 until the following 7 January. There is no mention of his stay in extant Wells documents. We know of it only from the fourteen entries dated at Wells in the Patent Rolls. The Archbishop of Canterbury, Simon de Meopham, who also wanted to spend Christmas at Wells that year, had to stay instead in the bishop's manor at Wiveliscombe, before going on to Exeter.

### The Black Death

No sooner was the work on the central tower and quire completed than the Black Death struck, first in the West of England in 1348. It has been calculated on the basis of the bishop's register that 47.6 per cent of Somerset clergy died and were replaced during those few months. It must be remembered that (a) most registers are incomplete, owing to an occasional oversight; and (b) for some clergy who died no replacement could be found. So the actual mortality was probably even higher than 47.6 per cent. The same authority criticizes the bishop for remaining throughout this period on his manor of Wiveliscombe, instead of busying himself actively in the towns, such as Bristol. But Bristol was in the diocese of Worcester, where his interference would doubtless have been resented: it would certainly have complicated, rather than solved, the problem. As it was, on his country manor, where food would be more easily available for the bishop and his staff, they achieved some amazingly efficient administration in replacing so many clergy who had died, and so ministering to the bodies and souls of the people.

Certainly Ralph of Shrewsbury's popularity throve on it.
When he was appointed, he was not greatly liked; but when he
died, very old and infirm, in 1363, he was revered and loved,
judging by the great total of contributions made over several
years in the money-box by his tomb.

While the Chapter finished the quire the bishop built Vicars'
Hall, completed at the end of 1348 (when the Black Death was
at its worst in Somerset), and started on the scheme for the
Vicars' Close. He also, after the plague was over, built the
Choristers' House (see p. 72).

The next phase of building was under the famous William
Wynford, appointed master mason in 1365. This included the
reconstruction of the interior west end round the west window
and the west gallery; completion of the quire aisle vaults
towards the west; the stone screens in the transept, including
that for the famous clock; and the south-west tower, towards
which Bishop Harewell provided two-thirds of the cost, and
two bells, Great Harewell and Little Harewell. Later the metal
of Little Harewell, and much else besides (including the clock
bell) had to be added to Great Harewell, the tenor bell, to
make it strong enough for its size. It is still known as Harewell
($56\frac{1}{4}$ cwt/2,857.5 kg). Soon after that the Early English lancets
in transepts and nave were given Perpendicular tracery of
Wynford's design, and a scheme of stained glass decoration
was begun in the same windows.

Richard II and his Queen, Anne of Bohemia, visited Wells
shortly after their marriage in 1382 and jointly donated one
mark (13s. 4d.), as we know from the accounts. Nothing else is
known about their visit.

In his will Nicholas Bubwith, Bishop 1407–24, bequeathed
money for the building of the library over the whole length of
the east cloister; the raising of the north-west tower in exact
imitation of Wynford's south-west tower, and a fund for the
improvement of the roads and bridges of Somerset, on condition that the library was finished first. He died in November
1424, and work on the library or completing it, cannot have
begun before the spring of 1425. Then followed the north-
west tower, which is a mere shell re-using a lot of old stone; it
was referred to in one of the later account-rolls as 'the rotten
tower'. The money allocated for the improvement of Somerset roads and bridges was diverted—cynics say nothing has
been done yet to improve them—to the erection of the
Almshouse, incorporating the city's Guildhall, at the bottom

*Thomas Bekynton, bishop 1443–65. He had his tomb prepared 15 years before his death.*

of Chamberlain Street, begun in 1436.

In 1443 Thomas Bekynton, a Somerset man, became bishop. As Secretary to King Henry VI he had supervised the building of Eton College, and had also been concerned with the building of Lincoln College, Oxford. With the cathedral church itself not much remained to be done, but a great deal in the precincts. The twelve houses, known still as 'The New Works', on the north side of the market-place, and three adjoining Brown's Gate in Sadler Street, were built by him (p. 162) and given to the Dean and Chapter to provide them with a fixed annual income from rents for the maintenance of the cathedral. (These are now taken, with all other cathedral endowments, by the Church Commissioners.) He made additions to the Palace, including the wing in which the present bishop lives; and the four gateways: the Bishop's Eye, Penniless Porch, Brown's Gate and, last of all, the Chain Gate. He gave the town its first water supply. Work on the present west cloister range, replacing an earlier, narrower one, was started by him, but not vaulted and completed until about 1480.

Money left at the discretion of the executors was used to heighten the chimneys of Vicars' Close (see p. 176 below).

Bekynton's successor, Robert Stillington, visited the diocese for only 3½ weeks in the whole of his tenure of the see for 25 years. Much of the rest of the time he spent in prison for one reason or another. But during his one and only visit to Wells as bishop, he ordered or approved the complete and luxurious rebuilding of the Lady Chapel by the cloister. During his episcopate work continued on the south cloister, first of all under Hugh Sugar, the Treasurer, who was Stillington's Vicar-general; and then after Sugar's death in 1489, under Thomas Harris, the new Treasurer, until work was finally completed in 1508. There have been no additions since then to the cathedral buildings, though some loss and much repair.

Stillington's Lady Chapel lasted only from 1488 until 1552, when Sir John Gates was allowed to take the lead roof, to help refill Edward VI's treasury, on condition that he utterly removed the whole building, leaving the site 'fayre and playne'. After the recent excavations (1978–80) the surface of the ground was deliberately lowered, so as to leave the foundations of Stillington's chapel visible. The reason for the wholesale removal of this enormous chapel, larger than the quire, was because, with the passing of the Act of 1547 abolishing chantries, the cathedral lost its main source of income—payments for obits; and being faced at that time with enormous charges for repairs to the lead roof of the main church, anything removeable—memorial brasses, candlesticks, etc.—was sold in an effort to meet the bill for repairs. Even so the Fabric account for 1549–50 showed a deficit. This co-incided with the Reformation, when ornaments would have been swept away in any case.

Probably it was at the same time that All Saints' Chapel, also known as Cokeham's Chantry, was demolished. It stood in the middle of the cloister garth (Palm Churchyard)—either liter-ally in the middle, where the yew tree is now, or on the north side projecting, as it were, from the south nave aisle. Suffragan bishops were not allowed to hold ordinations or institutions in the quire: that was the diocesan bishop's prerogative. Suffra-gans used either the Lady Chapel by the cloister or this Chapel of All Saints, which is first mentioned in 1348 and lastly in 1538; or, in one case, the private chapel of the suffragan's own house.

When we try to look at the impact made by people and

events at Wells upon the history of the country at large, there is very little we can find. The families of three of Becket's murderers—Brito, Fitzurse and Traci—had close connections with Somerset, and by way of expiation contributed lands to form prebends of the cathedral (all long since swallowed by the Church Commissioners). A member of the family of the fourth murderer, de Morevill, appears, but only as a witness, in 1239.

Because so many of the mediaeval bishops of Bath and Wells held high office as Chancellor and so on under the king, royal correspondence in the Close and Patent Rolls was not infrequently issued from Wells. But this had little impact, if any, either on the cathedral or the populace.

While Bekynton was bishop (1443–65), Wells harboured some of the chief humanists of the day: Andrew Holes, Archdeacon of Wells; Adam Moleyns, Archdeacon of Taunton, and others. From 1472 to 1498 John Gunthorpe, another leader of the Renaissance in England, was dean. Musically Wells had no small reputation at that time, as Richard Hygons's five-part setting of *Salve Regina* in the Eton choirbook must prove. At the same time as Hygons was organist, Henry Abyndon, who in 1464 had gained the earliest Mus.B. degree at Cambridge, was succentor at Wells until 1497, when he was followed by Robert Wydowe, the earliest known B.Mus. of Oxford, who from being succentor 1497–1500, rose to canon residentiary and subdean in 1500 until his death in 1505. In his *Anglica Historia* of 1534 the Italian, Polydore Virgil speaks of the Wells Chapter:

'There flourished a famous college of priests, men of honest behaviour and well learned; wherefore I account it no small worship that I myself, fourteen years Archdeacon of Wells, was elected one of that college.'

In the spring of 1470 Warwick ('the Kingmaker') and Clarence, having been pronounced traitors, were fleeing to the West Country, pursued by Edward IV. At Wells Edward IV and his brother, 'false, fleeting, perjur'd Clarence', seem to have been reconciled. Together they presumably stayed at the Bishop's Palace, while Warwick was at the Deanery. The king made an offering of 10 shillings in the cathedral, and the Duke and Duchess of Clarence 5 shillings each. The Earl of Warwick, plainly disgruntled, gave only 5 pence, and that was in the Dean's chapel. The king, we know, was in Wells on

Wednesday, 11 April, when he issued a document there, but there is nothing to indicate that the bishop, Stillington, was here at that time.

In 1497 something of the same nature happened when Henry VII was directing the capture of Perkin Warbeck at Taunton. On his way there he had to stay at the Deanery, together with John Morton, the aged Archbishop of Canterbury and Chancellor of England, because the Palace had been left empty so long. The bishop, Oliver King, although enthroned (by proxy) in the previous year had not yet visited Wells. The Palace was probably unfurnished, since Bishop Fox, if he ever visited the diocese at all, had never lived there; Stillington literally only for a day or two: otherwise for his few days' visit in 1476 he had stayed in his manor of Wookey. So the Palace had been virtually empty for thirty years. But the bishop came specially on this occasion and welcomed the king on his arrival on Saturday, 30 September 1497. The king spent Sunday in Wells and moved on to Glastonbury on Monday, 2 October. During that year (we have only the accounts to go by) the king made three separate donations in the cathedral amounting to £1; while Archbishop Morton gave 3s. 4d.

## After the Reformation

After the Reformation several of the deans were laymen with little, if any, interest in the cathedral apart from their stipends, which enabled them to carry out state appointments as ambassadors or civil servants.

One of the most zealous deans was William Turner, Doctor of Medicine, who had special leave of absence issued by Edward VI to allow him to preach the Gospel in any part of the kingdom. This may incidentally have enabled him to pursue his special interest in botany, for he wrote the earliest English *Herbal*, based largely on his own observation and discoveries, while earlier books on the subject had been merely translations of foreign books.

Certainly there were conscientious deans, but none of earthshaking importance. Walter Ralegh, however, a nephew of the explorer, made himself famous by being murdered by his gaoler under the Commonwealth in 1646, for refusing to show him a letter he was writing to his wife.

Ralph Bathurst, Dean 1670–1704, held the Deanery longer than anybody else at Wells. He was also President of Trinity College, Oxford, over the same period, a scientist of no mean

### Of Oxyacantha.

Berberis Oxyacantha.

Doth not agre wᵗ our berberis. Firſt our berberis buſhe looketh not lyke a wilde pere tre/for it is rather a buſhe then a tre/ for in all the places that euer J ſaw it in/ it neuer roſe vp to þ bygnes of a tre. The berries of barberis and of the Myrt tre ar not in proportion ⁊ figure lyke. for the berberis beris ar great in the myddes ⁊ ſmall at bothe þ endes / after the maner of a log eg. Suche faſſhō of figure is not in a Mirt berry. Dioſcorides ſemeth to geue one berry Oryacatha/ but one ſtone or kirnel/but euery berri of berberies hath iiij.at þ leſte/wherefore it is not lyke that our berberis ſhould be Oryacantha. Thus muche J had marked before J ſaw Matthiolus. But after that J ſaw Matthiolus J learned of hym an other reſon to proue that our berberis cold not be Oryacatha/ which was thys. Dioſcorides deſcribyng the former kynde of Meſpilus or medler tre/ ſayeth that it hath a lefe lyke vnto Oryacantha. But the former kynde of Meſpilus/as Theophraſtus witneſſeth hath indented leues/⁊ in the vtter moſte parte lyke vnto the leues of perſely. But there is no lykenes betwene the leues of berberis ⁊ of perſely: wherefor berberis can not be Oryacantha. The forenamed Matthiolus holdeth þ our haw tre or whyte thorne tre is Oryacantha. But when as our haw thorn tre leſeth hys leues euery yere/⁊ Theophraſt in hys firſt booke de hiſtoria Plantarū ⁊ in þ xv. chapter reherſeth Oryacantham amongeſt the trees þ haue grene leues all the yere. J can not ſe how þ our comō hawthorn ſhoulde be Oryacantha. How that Matthiolus will anſwer to thys J can not tell/ but J haue no other ſhift ſauing thys. Jn Summerſet ſhyre about ſix myles from Welles/in þ parke of Gaſſenberry there is an hawthorne which is grene all the wynter/as all they þ dwell there about do ſtedfaſtly holde. Jf Oryacantha be any kynde of hawthorn/it muſt be þ kynde which abydeth grene all þ hole yere throw. But if that our hawthorne be not Oryacantha/ as J ſuppoſe playnly that it is a kynde of it/it is Spina alba in Columella as God willyng here after J intend to proue.

### The vertues of Oxyacantha.

He berries of Oryacantha taken ether in meat or drynke/ ſtop þ ſlix of the belly and the iſſhue of weomen. The roote of the ſame laide to emplaſterwyſe pulleth out prickes and ſhiuers.

*Out of Galene in hys booke of ſimple medicines.*

Ory⸗

A page from the Herbal compiled by William Turner, Dean of Wells, known as the 'father of English botany'. Here, 10 lines from the bottom, he refers to the Glastonbury thorn.

reputation, and an early Fellow of the Royal Society. William Levinz, also a doctor and Fellow of the Royal Society, was subdean and canon residentiary, 1682–98, while being President of St John's College, Oxford. But the longest-lasting dignitary was Robert Creyghton [II], precentor from 1674 to 1734. He was the son of Robert Creyghtone [I] who had been treasurer of the cathedral, 1632–60, chaplain to Charles II in exile, Dean of Wells 1660–70, and Bishop of Bath and Wells, 1670–72. Frederick Beadon was canon residentiary 1812–79, and also chancellor of the cathedral, 1823–79. He died 'in harness' at the age of 101.

While bishops immediately before the Reformation, as has already appeared, tended to be absent from both Wells and the diocese generally, after the Reformation they were more conscientious. Thomas Fuller in his famous book *The Worthies of England*, 1662, observed that there had never been a Saint Arthur, and he proposed Arthur Lake, Bishop of Bath and Wells 1616–26, as the most eligible candidate for the vacancy. This was on the basis of his generosity and humility. For canonization he would be a worthy rival of Thomas Ken, Bishop of Bath and Wells 1685–91, whose life and example brought him far more into the public eye and regard. James II attempted to repeal the Act of Uniformity unconstitutionally and so stirred up the opposition of the Archbishop of Canterbury and six other bishops (including Ken). Instead of acting lawfully, he locked them in the Tower of London; but had to release them amid much public rejoicing, because he had not a legal foot to stand on. Three years later, after James II had abandoned the throne without abdicating, and William of Orange and Mary his wife (daughter of James II) had succeeded to the throne, Thomas Ken refused to take the oath of allegiance to them, as he was required to do as a public figure, on the grounds that he had already sworn allegiance to James II, who had gone into voluntary exile, but had not abdicated. Ken was therefore deprived of his bishopric, as was to be expected, though a little tact and compromise on both sides might have saved the situation. But he did not go, until at last forced to in 1691. Even then he continued to sign himself Bishop of Bath and Wells until his friend, George Hooper, was offered the bishopric in 1704. In modern times the most outstanding and, with Edward Henderson (1960–75), the best loved bishop was Lord Arthur Hervey, Bishop 1869–94.

The nineteenth-century restoration of the Lady Chapel and

*This coffee-pot belonged to the celebrated Thomas Ken, bishop 1685–91.
The arms engraved on it are those of William Hawkins, his nephew, who
inherited it.*

nave of the cathedral began in a conservative spirit under Benjamin Ferrey as architect and Edmund Goodenough as Dean, 1831–45, who also started the series of Minute Books of Chapter meetings. The restoration was continued more drastically in the quire, with Salvin as architect, under Richard Jenkyns, Dean 1845–54, who was at the same time Master of Balliol. The major restoration of the West Front, 1870–74, was taken under the vigorous chairmanship of the Earl of Cork and Orrery (Lord Lieutenant), when G H S Johnson (also a Fellow of the Royal Society) was Dean. He disliked Wells and lived at Clifton or Weston-super-Mare. He did not always attend West Front committee meetings ('I knew nothing would be decided'); and he had a low opinion of Ferrey, the architect in charge. ('Mr Ferrey is rather a Bungler!') Now Ferrey is thought to have done an extremely good job, considering the difficulties facing him.

The personal side of cathedral life, and the Cathedral School, flourished under Dean Plumptre (1881–91). Under his successor, Thomas Jex-Blake, much stained glass was added, and he gave first editions of some of Ruskin's works to the Cathedral Library. Then in 1911 that great scholar, Joseph Armitage Robinson, who had been born at Keynsham in Somerset where his father was vicar, was transferred from the Deanery of Westminster to Wells. His great scholarship, together with his energy in restoring to use the side chapels, repairing and discussing the ancient glass, and many other things, helped in some cases by the financial aid of wealthy friends, served to make this obscure cathedral better known. His energy has been matched by that of the present Dean, Patrick Mitchell, but it is too soon fully to evaluate his achievement. He is at any rate the first Dean of Wells to be given the Freedom of the City.

# Chapter Two

# A WALK ROUND THE OUTSIDE OF THE CATHEDRAL

THE CATHEDRAL GREEN, facing the West Front, is the obvious starting-point. The Green itself was by statute of 1243 allocated as the lay cemetery; canons were to be buried in the Palm Churchyard (Cloister Garth); vicars choral in the Camery (East of the Cloisters). Across the Green ran a line of elm trees, said to be the earliest recorded deliberate planting of an avenue in England. At least two recent books have suggested that the present row of lime trees along the southern border of the Green is descended from those early elms; but such cross-breeding is impossible.

*The West Front*

The West Front itself dates from about 1230. The plinth may be slightly earlier, for it appears to have been built together with the western part of the nave, under Adam Lock, the master mason, who died in 1229. The more decorative work above was probably designed by Thomas Norreys, one of the signatories to Lock's will, having obviously worked under him. The Front itself, excluding the towers and the central gable is exactly twice as wide as it is high. This is typical of the simple geometry used in the design of this cathedral.

The stone, of which almost the whole cathedral is built, is Inferior Oolite from Doulting, 8 miles (12 km) away. 'Inferior' does not mean 'worse': rather it means that it comes from the stratum below the Greater Oolite, which is Bath stone.

Doulting is both harder and coarser than Bath stone. The quarry belonged to Glastonbury Abbey; and the Abbey itself and many local churches and other buildings were built of Doulting stone. In modern times it has been used for the interior dressings of Guildford Catheral and also for the extension of Bury St Edmunds.

Throughout the West Front vertical shafts, originally of blue lias from Street, $6\frac{1}{2}$ miles ($10\frac{1}{2}$ km) away, adorned the niches, giving the polychrome effect beloved by the later thirteenth century. In the restoration of 1870–4 Benjamin Ferrey replaced many of these in Kilkenny marble, and the stone weathered well, and is now an almost perfect match. It is difficult even for an expert to tell from ground-level whether any particular shaft is of lias or Kilkenny marble. So more replacements, wherever necessary, were made in the recent restoration, using Kilkenny marble, but there is still some blue lias there.

(When the cathedral of Chartres was being rebuilt in 1145, we are told that

> 'men began in their humility to drag carts and wagons for the building of the cathedral.'

In 1976 volunteers in Wells, partly in the same spirit as the men of Chartres and partly as a 'stunt' to publicize the cathedral appeal, offered to charter lorries, and load, fetch and unload new shafts from Kilkenny and bring them over on the Fishguard boat. But they were assured of the unions' objections, and that this might provoke a national transport strike. So what seemed a good idea had to be discarded.)

The statues, mostly carved between 1230 and 1250, are placed round the immense buttresses, and on three sides of the north tower, with no particular emphasis on the doorways, as on the Continent. In fact, the doorways are very small. The doors leading into the aisles have been described as 'mouseholes'. Even the central door is small and was used only for processions on a few special occasions in the church's year.

In England, in most major churches and many parish churches, the main entrance is by a north or south door, leaving the west door (if any) permanently locked. This is said, but not always accepted, to be because the English people, being humble, do not like to approach the altar direct; and also because the devil cannot go round corners. If these reasons are not sufficient, it may be at Wells because of the prevailing west wind blowing across the Atlantic, which frequently produces a whirlwind outside the West Front and very unpleasant conditions there at Kill-Canon Corner. For beyond Sadler Street, with its row of houses facing the Green, the ground falls away to Bridgwater Bay, the Bristol Channel and the high seas. It may be for the same reason that the western towers were placed outside the line of the aisles. Such an arrangement is by no means unique. At least 17 other churches have been listed where this was done. At Wells the idea may have been borrowed from Old St Paul's in London.

The identification of the statues is virtually impossible. An attempt was made by Cockerell (1851), based almost wholly on guesswork and without regard for the attributes of the statues themselves. A much more reasoned attempt at identifying them piecemeal was made by Lethaby and St John Hope in 1904, but this did not consider the overall design. More recently the present Dean, Patrick Mitchell, has recognized what is undoubtedly a Gospel procession at the north-east corner of the northern tower (p. 45 below), and has seen the *Noah's Ark* of Hugh of St Victor as the basis of the general scheme of the whole Front; but it is difficult to identify every single statue on this basis. It may well be that Elias of Dereham, the comptroller of the building work at Salisbury, as well as canon of Wells and friend and steward of Bishop Jocelyn, may have given the master mason or the sculptors the general scheme of iconography, on the basis of which they produced so many anonymous bishops, kings, queens, knights in armour, other ecclesiastics; just as Henry III gave 'five statues of Kings' (unidentified), surplus to requirements at Westminster Abbey, to the canons of St Martin-le-Grand, who were building a Lady Chapel. Recently the whole façade has been brilliantly described as 'Pure adoration without words'.

William Worcestre gave the only mediaeval description of the West Front when he wrote in 1480:

> 'Note that at the north-west corner of the cathedral are three great buttresses with three tiers of great statues from the Old Testament. And on the west front of the church are six great tall buttresses, 6 feet in width and projecting about 3 yards, with three tiers of great carved statues from the New Testament; and at the north-west corner

*OPPOSITE: The north-east corner of the base of the north-west tower with its thirteenth-century sculpture. In the centre of the bottom row is the Gospel procession; and the four Marys (pp. 44–5) are on the right.*

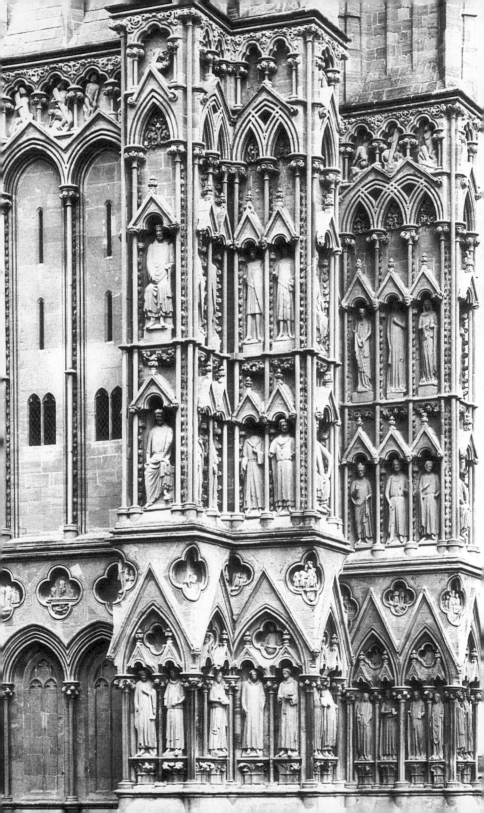

*Memorial inscription carved at the time of the Black Death on a buttress of the West Front.*

of this church are two great buttresses about 60 feet in
height, with three tiers of sculpture with great statues
from the New Testament.'

This does not help us very much. He says 'north-west corner'
twice: one of these should presumably be 'south-west', but
which? The Old Testament quatrefoils are on the south side,
with ecclesiastics above. On the north side are the New
Testament scenes in quatrefoils, the Four Marys and the Gospel
procession. A plan with statues numbered in series from top to
bottom and left to right can be bought in the Cathedral Shop.
This numbering is still used and is used on the following pages,
but the identification, based on Lethaby and St John Hope, is
now superannuated, if not superseded.

Within the soffit of the great west door there is a Madonna
and Child, to which new heads were added by A J Ayres in
1970. This addition of new parts to mediaeval figures caused an
uproar in the Press in 1973 (three years after it was done), as a

result of which the proposal also to add heads to the figures of Christ and his Mother in the Coronation of the Virgin group above was abandoned. Instead, the new dean, Patrick Mitchell, and the Chapter resolved on a complete and long-needed restoration of the whole West Front, in which no new parts at all were to be added to old statues; if absolutely necessary, a few figures might be taken down, preserved in museum conditions, and new replacements provided on the Front. With the help of an immediate grant of £30,000 from the Pilgrim Trust, work began on the statues on the east face of the northern tower, various methods being tried experimentally. As a result of this, it was decided to use Robert Baker's lime-poultice method, already used successfully on the statues on the north face of the north transept of Merton College chapel, Oxford. So by October 1976, when a national appeal was launched for £1,300,000 to cover the cost of the restoration of the West Front as well as of the high vaults of nave and transepts, those responsible knew exactly what they wanted to do and how to do it. This was in a period of extreme inflation, and it was very soon clear that far more money would be needed. But so successful was the work and so favourably reported on by experts, that the second million pounds was raised without much difficulty. The actual work of conservation of the West Front took twelve years, as originally predicted, from March 1975 to June 1986 inclusive.

The following figures were renewed: the figure of Christ in the topmost gable, with seraphim on either side (nos. 1, 2, 3), carved by David Wynne. The fifteenth-century figure of Bishop Bubwith on the tower built by his bequest was very badly decayed, and was replaced by a new figure by Edwin Russell, 1980. A seated king (199), being the lower figure facing west on the north buttress of the West Front, was replaced by Simon Verity, 1980. The upper figure (160), facing west, on the buttress south of the great west window, a king, was replaced by Derek Carr. These last two kings had been intensively repaired in the Victorian restoration with cement, which had reacted badly on the original stone, causing it to revert almost to sand.

Starting from the very bottom: on the west face of the plinth of the buttress north of the central door, is an inscription in fine writing:

PVR ⠂ LALME ⠂ JOHAN ⠂
DE ⠂ PVTTENIE ⠂ PRIEZ ⠂
ET ⠂ TREZE ⠂ IVRS ⠂ DE ⠂

The last line is missing and, to rhyme, scan and make sense, has been conjectured as: PARDON ⠂ AVEREZ ⠂

'Pray for the soul of John of Pitney and receive thirteen days' indulgence.'

A John of Pitney was chantry priest at Crewkerne in South Somerset from 1345. He died in December 1348, when the Black Death was at its worst. It is assumed that a sculptor was asked to carve a tombstone for him. As no stone was available, the sculptor grabbed a buttress and started to incise that until he too died; and the inscription remains unfinished.

Only four statues (339 and 340 on the north, and 382 and 383 on the south) on the bottom row remain facing west, but the bottom row on the north face and north-east corner is almost complete. In Richard Newcourt's drawing, engraved

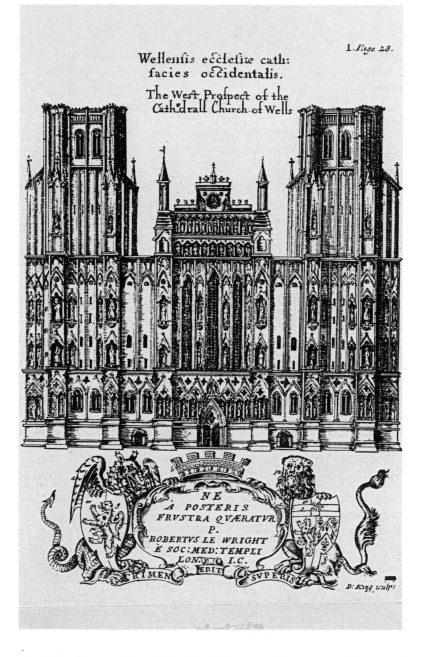

The West Front, as drawn by Richard Newcourt of Somerton and engraved by Daniel King for Dugdale's Monasticon Anglicanum, vol. I, 1655.

Over the great west door, the inserted niche with the beautifully carved, but now headless, figure of Christ crowning His Mother. Above, left, the figure of St Matthew looks towards the series of New Testament scenes. On the right is clearly seen the Creation of Eve from Adam's side near the beginning of the Old Testament series. The lower row of quatrefoils contained the busts of angels (some still undergoing repair) and the holes through which the choir sang 'All glory, laud and honour . . .' on Palm Sunday.

by Daniel King, for Dugdale's *Monasticon Anglicanum*, volume I (1655), the figures are shown complete. If Newcourt's drawing was authentic—he lived at Somerton, and so ought to know—it means the damage was not done by the Roundhead soldiers in the civil war: Monmouth's rebels in 1685 must have been responsible. They, we know, were drunk and caused much damage, and are said to have levered the statues off with their pikes.

Next above this row are the heads and shoulders of angels in quatrefoils, rising above clouds and each carrying some special object, such as a crown, a scroll, a sudary, a mitre or a book. In the niches behind the angels under the great west window can be seen holes, through which choristers behind the lower holes, vicars choral using the upper row, sang on the occasion of great festivals—notably Palm Sunday—when the west door was used. Because the holes are splayed in the normal way inside, unlike megaphones, it was at first doubted whether this tradition was true. But experiment proved that the back wall of the interior passage acts as a sounding-board from which the sound is reflected and collected within the splay of the holes, and released loudly, just as with a megaphone.

The West Fronts of many other churches have similar holes, and a mediaeval drawing of the Temple in Jerusalem depicts it with identical rows of holes. At the time of writing these holes at Wells are exposed, because some of the angels are carved out of a softer white stone which cannot be water-washed for fear of damage, so have had to be removed for slow and delicate treatment. They will be replaced after being treated.

Round the figures of the Coronation of the Virgin over the west door, small holes can be seen from the ground. It was conjectured at one time that these were bullet-holes caused by rebels trying to knock off the heads by musket-fire. But when examined at close quarters they were seen to be arranged in double arcs of two concentric circles, and wooden plugs were found in some of the holes; so clearly these holes must have held the fixings of a metal inscription over the sculptured group. Attempts at discovering the wording of the inscription to conform to the positions of the fixings of the letters have proved unsuccessful.

It is thought that the niche containing the Coronation of the Virgin was put in *c*.1260, probably after work on the West Front had been completed for the time being. The niche is an awkward shape, and appears to have taken the place of an

earlier, slightly narrower niche, which probably had a triangular top, like the other niches in that row, though possibly
larger, as on the West Front of Salisbury. The insertion of the
present wide niche has disturbed and tilted the bench of St
Matthew in the adjoining quatrefoil to the north.

The upper row of quatrefoils to the north of the Coronation
of the Virgin depict, first of all, St Matthew, represented by his
symbol, a winged man (as described in the *Book of Revelation*)
with a halo. His head is turned toward his right, and he also
points to the series of New Testament scenes, almost all of
which are recorded in his Gospel, which rests on the eagle-
lectern, clearly resembling the one drawn by Villard de
Honnecourt in his Notebook of *c*.1250.

265–6. *two missing.*
264. The Nativity.
259–63. *five missing.*
258. The Return from
Egypt.
257. Christ disputing with
the Doctors.
256. John the Baptist.
255. John the Baptist
preaching.
253–4. *two missing.*
252. Christ in the synagogue
of Nazareth expounds the
scriptures from the scroll
held across His knees.
251. Christ at supper in
Simon's house. The
sinner-woman, Mary, kneels
in front.
250. The feeding of the five
thousand (?).
249. Christ talking to a
group of people.
248. The Transfiguration. In
the foreground Peter, James
and John lie prostrate before
the figures of Christ (with

halo), Moses and Elijah (both
now headless).
247. The Entry into
Jerusalem on Palm Sunday.
Christ riding on an ass
approaches an elaborate
gateway. Figures with
palm-branches stand about,
above and below, and three
peer out of windows.
246. Judas and the High
Priest. On the right Judas
(headless), with a devil
prompting him from behind,
in discussion with the High
Priest, who is wearing a
horned mitre. On the left,
someone gets the thirty
pieces of silver out of a
chest.
245. The Last Supper. St
John reclines in front of Our
Lord. Judas kneels in front to
receive the sop. On the table
are winecups and bread-rolls;
a large flask and additional
rolls in a basket under the
table.

*OPPOSITE: Christ's entry into Jerusalem on the first Palm Sunday.*

244. *missing*.

243. Christ before the High Priest. A crowded scene.

242. Christ before Pilate. The figure of Christ having been destroyed, the two side-pieces, which originally fitted perfectly, seem to have been brought together at a previous restoration.

241. Three men wearing tunics and tight hose. The last man has his right hand on the shoulder of the man in front.

240. Christ bearing His cross.

239. *missing*.

238. The Resurrection. Christ stepping out of His tomb. In the background two angels stand with wings outspread. Below are three Roman soldiers, asleep.

237. The Ascension. The figure in front, wearing a long gown, is the Virgin Mary, nearly always shown present at the Ascension in mediaeval art.

The quatrefoils in the same row on the south side of the Coronation of the Virgin have scenes from the first part of the book of *Genesis*.

268. *missing*. Presumably the missing figure was that of Moses, traditional author of the first five books of the Bible, to correspond to St Matthew on the north side.

269. The Creation of Adam.

270. Creation of Eve. While Adam lies asleep against a rock, God the Father lifts Eve out of his side. The composition closely resembles that in the Winchester Bible.

271. God leads Adam and Eve into the garden and warns them against tasting the fruit of the Tree of the Knowledge of Good and Evil.

272. Adam eats the apple. Adam and Eve cover themselves with leaves. At the top of the larger tree at the back the Serpent bites another apple.

273. The Lord God walks in the garden in the cool of the evening.

274. (Expulsion from Eden, *missing*. Only a fragment of a tree remains.)

275. Adam delves and Eve spins.

*Noah building the ark. The clinker-built boat is not just a block of stone, but properly hollowed out. (Photograph taken before conservation.)*

*The four Marys. On the right, Mary, the mother of Jesus, wears a chasuble.*

In the lower row of tall figures above, most of those immediately to the north of the great west window are martyrs, represented mainly by Anglo-Saxon kings and queens standing upon small crouching figures of those who betrayed or murdered them on earth. Right and left of the centre light are King Solomon and the Queen of Sheba (216, 215). Her visit to Solomon in Jerusalem was regarded as the prototype of the Journey of the Magi to worship the infant Christ, and this, in turn, was regarded allegorically as the attraction of the gentiles to the Christian church. From here southwards, on both tiers, nearly all the figures are of ecclesiastics, one Pope, several bishops, mitred abbots, monks and hermits.

The statues on the north face are in the best state of preservation. Particularly worthy of notice are (a) the four Marys (332–5): Mary Cleopas; Mary Magdalen or Mary of Bethany, carrying the alabaster box of ointment; Mary, the mother of James and Joses; and Mary, the mother of Our Lord, here shown wearing a chasuble; and (b) the series of statues at the north-east corner previously mentioned, making up the Gospel procession. The figures are arranged in pairs: thurifer and book-bearer alternately, as in the procession of canons at Amiens: (322) a deacon wearing a long surplice, with his stole crossing from left shoulder to right side, and a maniple hanging from his left arm. In his left hand he held the chains of the censer against his chest, while with his right hand he held the censer itself. Deacon (323), wearing amice and girded alb, and stole crossing from left shoulder under his girdle to the right side. He holds the Gospel book, closed. (324) *missing*. Presumably this was the thurifer holding the censer and leaning forward to cense the book held by no. 325. Subdeacon (325), wearing cassock, amice and girded alb. He has a folded chasuble passing from his left shoulder to right side under his girdle. He holds the Gospel book open. Subdeacon (326), wearing amice and alb. He is presumably the thurifer, who has lowered the censer, which would in each case have been supplied in metal, like the other fittings. Acolyte (327), wearing amice and alb, in the act of closing the Gospel book in his left hand.

In the upper rows of large figures the following are especially to be noted: On the east face, St Eustace (118) fording a stream (the Nile), which comes up to his knees, and

*OVERLEAF, LEFT: A noble king's head. (Statue no. 178.)*

carrying his two children. On the north face: Knights in armour (123–126); and St Erkenwald (128). The painted embroidery on the saint's maniple is still clearly visible at close quarters, but from ground-level hidden by his body and the shadow of his niche.

In May 1257 the king sent for Simon of Wells to come to Westminster to make an image in gilt bronze over the tomb of the princess Katherine. He failed to make it; instead the king's goldsmith made an image of silver-gilt on a wooden core at much less cost. This Simon was perhaps the master carver at Wells, usually known as Simon the painter, who witnessed several documents at Wells, and whose son, Ralph, was a vicar choral of Wells by 1251. (The use of painter or *pictor* for 'sculptor' is attested by Martin le Payntour, who bequeathed two chisels and a 'hakhamer', unusual tools for a painter, to Richard the Mason of Lincoln.)

Even more accomplished than the actual statues are the patterns, always symmetrical but always different, in the tympana of the blind arches and in the spandrels of the arcades.

Running along the top of the ornamental Front are depicted figures pushing-up their coffin-lids and rising from their graves at the Great Resurrection. The whole design, with no two figures alike, is extremely vigorous and alive with movement. Above that must have been a receding crest on the wall, with seven set-offs, like that which remains on either side of the central gable; and as may still be seen over the south cloister wall facing the Bishop's Gatehouse. The set-off theme is continued in the lowest section of the fourteenth-century tower.

From close quarters it is apparent that there were two or more changes of design for the central gable. Certainly the two lower tiers of the gable seem to have been left empty of statues in the mid-thirteenth century, when money was exhausted through expenditure on litigation at Rome. The figures in these two rows date stylistically from the fifteenth century. The workmanship was poor and the stone of bad quality. Above are the Twelve Apostles, St Andrew, patron of the cathedral, standing slightly higher than the rest and holding his saltire, in the centre, next to his brother, St Peter. Below the

*PREVIOUS PAGE: Knight in armour, wearing a barrel helm. Even his eye-balls are carved, but can only be seen at close quarters from scaffolding. (Statue no. 123.) There are seven other knights in armour on the West Front.*

*The thirteenth-century wall of the south cloister, showing the rows of set-offs along the top, as well as on the buttresses.*

Apostles are the Nine Orders of Angels: Throne, Cherub, Seraph, Power, Virtue, Domination, Principality, Archangel, Angel. All are extremely badly weathered, and most of their attributes no longer recognizable. Behind them, however, their wings are in very good condition, still lavishly covered with crimson paint, but, recessed in their niches and in the shadow, hardly visible from the ground.

Above that, in the topmost gable, until 1984 there remained the lower half of a statue of Christ, originally carved out of two stones. The upper half had fallen at some time. Of this there is no record. The lower stone on which the knees, legs and feet were carved, still remained in good condition, with the top surface still flat. On stylistic grounds we may guess this to have been probably the remains of a thirteenth-century figure. It has been preserved, and was copied by David Wynne in the lower part of his new statue. In the southern niche adjoining, there had been the small square plinth of a missing figure. The plinth was recorded but removed in the 1870 restoration.

In 1983 to mark their golden jubilee the Friends of Wells Cathedral offered to supply a new statue of Christ for the central niche, by making a special collection among their members, without diminishing their annual payments out of subscriptions and legacies towards the maintenance of the fabric. Accordingly the Dean and Chapter commissioned David Wynne to make the statue of Christ for this position, and at the same time, at their own expense, the Seraphim in the side niches. For Dean Mitchell carried out three months' research at Oxford, as a result of which he discovered Hugh of St Victor's description which seemed exactly to fit this gable, in which the figure of Christ was described as flanked by seraphim, as recorded by Isaiah; and the two upper quatrefoils at the corners were, he said, the 'mouths of God' through which the 'Word may go forth from the Majesty' to the ends of the world. David Wynne accordingly carved the six-winged seraphim as he conceived them, and left the upper quatrefoils deliberately empty.

### The Western Towers

The large blind lancets in the lower part of the towers were not stone-filled until the actual towers were added above. During recent repairs to the West Front, when some of these stones had to be replaced, wooden plugs were found in the sides of these openings, showing that originally there had been a wooden lining, presumably with louvres. But the large blind lancets covering the ends of the aisles, and having sculpture in their tympana or apexes, are original.

The massive buttresses of the West Front indicate that great towers with spires were intended after the French pattern at the west end, as at Coutances, Lisieux and elsewhere in France. But when Bishop Harewell, c.1384, provided money towards the building of the south-west tower, the tall central tower had been built and crowned with a high spire after the English pattern. So the master mason, William Wynford, had to subordinate the western towers to the central one. Moreover, he plainly wished to preserve the strong horizontal emphasis already apparent in the West Front below, and indeed of the whole eleventh–twelfth-century cathedral. The tower parapets end on a straight line broken only by minute machicolations, which are typical of Wynford's work, as also are the double buttresses set diagonally, which Wynford seems to have derived from the earlier work on the corners of the eastern

*The statue of Christ in the gable of the West Front carved by David Wynne in 1985.*

transepts. Similar flat parapets occur also on the tower of St John's, Yeovil, which was also Wynford's work. The cathedral south-west tower was an innovation, inasmuch as all previous cathedral towers had been built to have spires. It is quite clear that no spires were intended at Wells, because there is no provision for them inside. It is true that the south-west tower has three corbels near the top on the north side, and three on the south side, designed to support the flat roof, and possibly also the bell-frame when bells were *swung*. But there are no corbels at all on the east and west sides, to take the terrific force of the prevailing wind. (When bells were *rung*, from Charles II's reign, a new bell-frame had to be made lower down.) The north-west tower, which had no bells, has similar corbels on north and south with struts on them to support the roof. A further reason for knowing that no spires were intended is that when Bishop Bubwith left very precise instructions in his will for works to be undertaken and paid for out of his bequests, he insisted that the north-west tower should be identical with the south-west, and said nothing about the addition of spires.

From the south-west tower arose the tradition of the famous spireless Somerset church towers. This tower contains the bells, the heaviest ring of ten in the world (Tenor: $56\frac{1}{4}$ cwt/ 2,857.5 kg: the sixth heaviest ringing bell). The way Wynford utilized and assimilated the giant buttresses, while at the same time producing twin towers in Perpendicular style, which are completely in keeping with the Early English bases, is masterly.

The earliest extant Fabric account, during the period when this tower was being built, shows that during May, 1391, William Wynford, the master mason, was present for three days, receiving 6d a day. At the same time the resident under-master, John Stone, was earning 3s. $8\frac{1}{2}$d a week, James the mason 3s. $2\frac{1}{4}$d and Thomas Holman 18d. There were no payments to any other workmen at Wells during this period. But at Doulting quarry Philip earned 20d a week, John Gylle 18d and a third man (William Wodeford, then Richard Baggeworthe, then Robert West) also earned 18d for a full week.

## The North Aisle

As we move round to the north side of the church, after looking at the statues on the north and east faces of the north tower, we can look at the aisle buttresses. First, it may be

*The heaviest ring of ten in the world. The bells are up, ready for ringing. The tenor bell is seen on the right.*

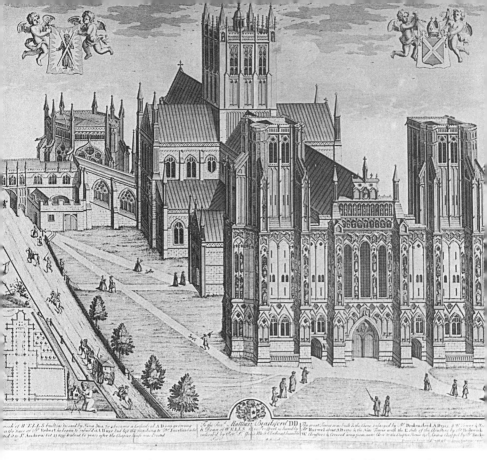

*An old print of c.1730, drawn by T Fourd and engraved by Toms, shows the cupola for the hour-bell built on top of the central tower c.1726, removed 1794; and the County Record Office against the Chain Gate, removed in 1874, when the ground was levelled.*

noticed that the lower string course frequently changes height. This is because the cathedral is built on the lower slope of Mendip, on land rising gradually: the string course was adjusted accordingly. But in 1874 the Cathedral Green was levelled both before the West Front and along the north side. Until this time there was a gradual and uneven slope down from the road to the north aisle wall. The sloping Green before the West Front produced an odd effect, which now that we are accustomed to the level Green, we can hardly appreciate. At the same time the late (date unknown) County Record Office, built on the north end of the Chapter House steps and occupying the archway, now filled with an iron gate, beneath the continuation of the steps leading to the Chain Bridge, was demolished. The old Record Office is clearly seen in Fourd's drawing engraved by Toms, c.1730, and other old prints.

The flying buttresses which transfer the thrust of the high nave vault to the buttresses along the aisle walls are covered by the aisle roofs. In the fourteenth-century extension of the presbytery the aisle roofs are much lower, and the flying buttresses, which are higher there, are exposed.

The set-offs on the nave buttresses are perplexing. The main buttresses above the plinth project between 2 feet 8 inches and 2 feet 9 inches. But the number of set-offs varies at the upper and lower weathering as follows:

| | S. buttress of N. Transept | 1st buttress of Nave aisle | 2nd buttress of Nave aisle | NORTH PORCH | 3rd buttress of Nave aisle | 4th buttress of Nave aisle | 5th buttress of Nave aisle |
|---|---|---|---|---|---|---|---|
| Set-offs at upper weathering | 2 | 3 | 2 | | 2 | 3 | 3 |
| Set-offs at lower weathering | 4 | 4 | 5 | | 3 | 5 | 5 |
| Projection: | 2ft 9ins | 2ft 9ins | 2ft 8¾ins | | 2ft 8ins | 2ft 8ins | 2ft 8½ins |

(On the south side of the nave, facing the Palm Churchyard, all the buttresses have plain weathering without set-offs, except the one on the west wall of the south transept, which has 3 set-offs on the upper weathering, none below.)

Below the high roof and below the aisle roofs the corbel-table is clearly seen. This was a formalized representation in stone of the ends of imaginary wooden rafters. At the southern end of the aisle corbel-table, on the east face of the north-west tower, and very close to the quatrefoil containing the carving of the Ascension, there is still in situ a small piece of the water-table, remaining from the time before the construction of the parapets, when the eaves still overhung the aisle walls.

These parapets at aisle and high roof level, of the same pattern as that surrounding the Lady Chapel (but wholly different from the Chapter House parapet), must have been made about 1320, certainly before the presbytery was extended eastwards.

In most major churches where the roof was of lead, parapets had to be made when the lead had been in position for about a hundred years. Because of the tendency of lead to creep downwards under its own weight, and thereby get thinner, it

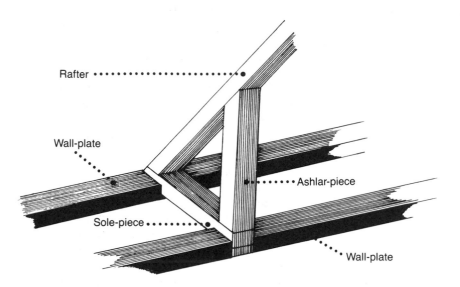

*The normal arrangement for fixing rafters to wall-plate.*

had to be taken down periodically, re-cast and replaced; or, to save time, replaced with new lead, for which the old lead was given in part-exchange. When this was done, if there were no parapet, immensely long ladders were necessary to extend from ground-level to the ridge of the high roof. The lead could be taken off only in very small sections because of its immense weight, and it had to be lowered, or rolled down the ladder all the way from top to bottom without a rest.

So in major churches having lead roofs, parapets were made for plumbers and others to work from; to rest their shorter ladders on; and to provide a resting-place from which the lead could be lowered by pulley in stages, to the aisle roof, the aisle parapet, and then straight down to the ground; and, even more important, to enable the new lead to be raised by stages to the high roof.

In order to create the parapet it was necessary to remove the wall-plate, cut off the ends of the rafters, and remove the small supporting timbers (sole-pieces and ashlar-pieces) which provide a right-angle fixing of the rafter-ends to the wall-plate. While this was done the rafters were supported by dead shores, which still remain inside the roof; without them, the rafters being unsupported when their ends had been cut off, the whole roof would collapse. The stone walls were then built up so as to provide the outside walkway, and also support the ends of the rafters on the inner edge of the walkway.

The purpose of the wall-plate was to prevent the rotting of the ends of rafters in contact with stone. But at Wells there are very few wall-plates: in almost every case, the ends of the rafters rest directly on the stone walls. Experience has shown at Wells that where there is a wall-plate the rafter-ends have rotted; but where there is no wall-plate and the rafter-ends rest directly on the stone they are free from rot.

### The North Porch

The North Porch is one of the most beautiful as well as interesting parts of the cathedral. It has been called 'perhaps the finest piece of architecture at Wells'. It is also one of the most problematical. Writers a hundred years ago considered it to be the earliest part of the present building. Pamela Tudor-Craig has pointed out the similarity of its intersecting arches and other features to those on the West Front. Dr Richard K Morris has also shown that some of the same mouldings occur on the West Front, and so far as is known nowhere else. Mr Jerry Sampson has demonstrated resemblances of the sculpture, particularly of the foliage, to carving at Glastonbury Abbey.

One could fill many pages with the description of this porch alone. The main entrance arch consists of a curious arrangement of free-standing ringed round shafts interspersed in an odd rhythm with keeled, snub-nosed attached shafts, all apparently without bases. But the bases have disappeared in an early restoration: they can still be seen behind the doors. These columns and shafts have richly-carved capitals: on the west side simply stiff-leaf foliage, but on the east the dramatic martyrdom of Edmund, King of East Anglia. On the left the king, wearing his crown, is transfixed by arrows fired by the Danes from both sides alternately, left and right. Then the wolf, coming from behind the door, discovers the king's head in a thicket and brings it to the king's retainers for burial.

The elaborate main arch has zigzag ornament combined with foliage; in its spandrels are two square carvings of unequal size[*], on the left David rescuing the lamb out of the lion's

* These are omitted from John Carter's careful drawing of 1794 in the possession of the Society of Antiquaries, but this must be an oversight, since they are present in Toms's engraving of c.1730.

*Inside the nave roof, dead shores were inserted temporarily c.1320, while the ends of the rafters were sawn off in order to construct the parapet. They are still there.*

*The martyrdom of King Edmund of East Anglia, as carved on the east side of the entrance to the North Porch. The Danes shot arrows into him from both sides. He was then beheaded, but a wolf retrieved his head from a thicket and brought it back to the king's men for burial.*

mouth (1 *Sam.* 17$^{34-6}$); on the right, a cockatrice, or other legendary beast. On each side of the gable there is a tall pinnacle. As always at Wells, pinnacles are set on top of buttresses, not just for decoration but to provide additional weight to stabilize the buttress.

The gable is filled with an arcade of blind lancets with small groups of sculpture, and three smaller lancet windows which light the parvise chamber containing the drawing-floor discovered by Dr John Harvey in 1954. This is one of the only two drawing-floors so far published. The master mason drew with a sharp point on a floor coated with plaster of paris his designs for mouldings, etc. in full. These showed up white against the grey background. If he did not like what he had drawn, he did not rub-out: he just left the faulty lines which soon reverted to dull grey, and drew again. When he was satisfied, he had moulds (or templates) made from them, usually out of thin oak or elm boards. These were then used by the masons to cut the stone accordingly. This floor must have been in use for three hundred years: consequently, many drawings overlap and are indecipherable. One very obvious design is visible, but the actual moulding has not been noted in the cathedral or precincts. (It might equally refer to one of the churches held by the Dean and Chapter, or to one of the bishop's former

manors.) Another is the full-size drawing of the rear windows of the Vicars' Close houses.

Inside the North Porch are deeply recessed arches formed by detached shafts and intersecting arches. The string course is bitten off at the end of each bay by the heads of serpents. (The sills of the windows in the Elder Lady Chapel at Bristol, on which a Wells craftsman was employed, are treated in a somewhat similar way, but by human or simian heads, or plain foliage.)

At the entrance doors to the cathedral are two small figures, one on either side. On the north side a canon bears a scroll with the words: *Intra in gaudium domini tui* (using the customary abbreviations): 'Enter thou into the joy of thy lord.' (*Mt.* 25[21,31]). And on the south, a bishop gives the blessing. The doors themselves belong to the first half of the thirteenth century, but have been re-faced with fifteenth-century tracery and mouldings on the outside. The outer porch doors are good eighteenth-century work. They were turned in 1939, so that the original outer face is now inside.

### The Central Tower

Near this point there is a good view of the central tower. This was raised as far as the lower rank of blind lancets, finishing 17 inches (43 cm) above the ridge of the roof, by about 1200; and a low temporary roof covered it. It was not until 1313 (when it is mentioned in a will) that work on it was resumed. Presumably a low tower was originally intended, about as high as its width, and with a low spire. But since by the fourteenth century England favoured tall central towers and spires, the tower itself was then built twice as high as it is broad. It is built with an inner and an outer skin, for strength combined with lightness; and also with stairs (the most economical form of buttressing) at each corner, just like Lincoln. Towards this work subscriptions to the Fraternity of Saint Andrew were sought in 1318. In January 1322 money was spent on 'covering' the tower, which could only be done at that time by the construction of a tall spire, in this case of timber covered with lead. We know this from the disaster of 1438–9 when the 'tower was burnt', 'the repair of the tower', 1439–40, and 'the time of the fall of the high tower'. *Turris* was the word for

*OPPOSITE: The impressive intersecting arches and serpent-like string-course of the North Porch.*

*'Enter thou into the joy of thy Lord.' A canon welcomes the visitor on his entry by the north door.*

'steeple', i.e tower + spire. Simon Simeonis commented in 1323 that the *turres* at Lichfield were not only very tall, but that they were built of stone. Corbels to support the spire exist inside the central tower on all four sides.

Before the fire each side of the tower had three pairs of very tall lancet openings. The lower portion which opened into the lantern, at that time open to the crossing beneath, was glazed. Sir Charles Nicholson noted the glazing-grooves when the tower was repaired in 1912. The upper part, where the bells hung, must have had louvres. After the building of the great scissor-arches inside the church, 1338–c.1348, to stabilize the

*The central tower, c.1200, consisted only of the lowest section decorated with blind lancets, reaching a short distance above the apex of the roof. In 1313 it was extended upwards, and the upper part re-designed after the spire was burnt down in 1438–9.*

tower, and as part of the same scheme interrupted by the Black Death, stone 'grids' were inserted inside the lantern to provide a square framework for the masonry, apparently designed by William Joy, master mason of the scissor-arches, who seems to have died in the Black Death. The Abbot of Glastonbury gave 40 loads of stone from the Abbey's quarry at Doulting in April 1354 for the building of the Choristers' House (p. 72 below), 20 loads for a purpose not specified in December 1354, and 50 loads in May 1356 for the repair of the tower. This would appear to be for the stone 'grids', just mentioned (see also p. 114).

After the spire was burnt down in 1438–9 drastic alterations were made to the outward appearance of the tower. The openings were filled with 'Somerset tracery', i.e. stone slabs with patterned openings, used locally in the Perpendicular period instead of louvres. Small windows were included. At the top of the tower, as if to compensate for the loss of the spire, twenty new pinnacles were added. The corner buttresses were carried straight up, forming niches at each corner for statues and bases for three secondary pinnacles surrounding each of the large fourteenth-century pinnacles, and blocking the water-chutes; two intermediate secondary pinnacles were added along each side, each 24 inches (60 cm) wide at base, which exactly filled one repeat of the parapet design. These pinnacles also stood over the earlier water-chutes, but holes were bored through, to enable the water to escape.

### The North Transept

Near the north-west corner of the north transept is a late face of the Wells clock. Two knights in armour strike the quarters. By their armour they can be dated *c*.1475. The face originally showed two sets of 12 hours for a.m. and p.m., according to the Old English system (see the interior clock-face), but was altered to the modern system *c*.1830. Over the clock-face is the painted inscription: NE QVID PEREAT: 'Let nothing be lost', referring both to the fabric of the church and to the passage of time. At the time this new face was added, operated by the old works inside of *c*.1390, the public were not allowed in the area

*OPPOSITE: The exterior clock-face: a later addition of c.1475, as shown by the style of armour worn by the two knights who strike the quarter-hours. The dial was renewed c.1830. Before that it showed two series of 12 hours—a.m. on the left and p.m. on the right, according to the old English system. (See interior dial.)*

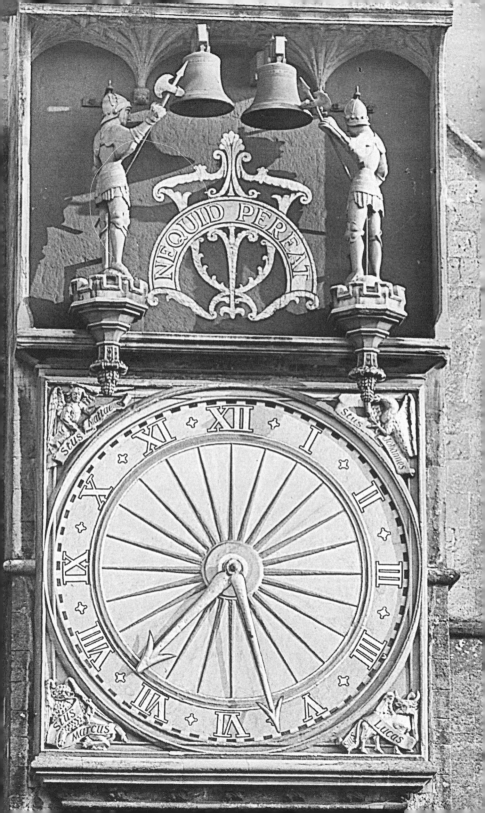

*The Chain Gate built by Bishop Bekynton, 1459–60, to enable the vicars choral to cross directly from their Hall to the cathedral for night-time services.*

of the Cathedral Green. The additional window made at that time in the upstairs kitchen of Vicars' Hall immediately opposite the clock, indicates that this face was put here for the benefit of the vicars assembled in their Hall. When the servants told them it was nearly time for service in the church, they would process across the Chain Bridge, completed in 1460, and down the stairs to take their place in quire, or in the appropriate chapel where the chaplain was due to say an obituary mass.

This gateway, commonly known as the Chain Gate, presumably because chains were regularly fastened across it to prevent the passage of unauthorized carts, was the last of the four gates built by Bishop Bekynton. Permission was given by the Dean and Chapter on 29 March 1459; and the vicars choral

*OPPOSITE: The octagonal Chapter House, begun c.1240, but not completed, after long delays, until c.1306.*

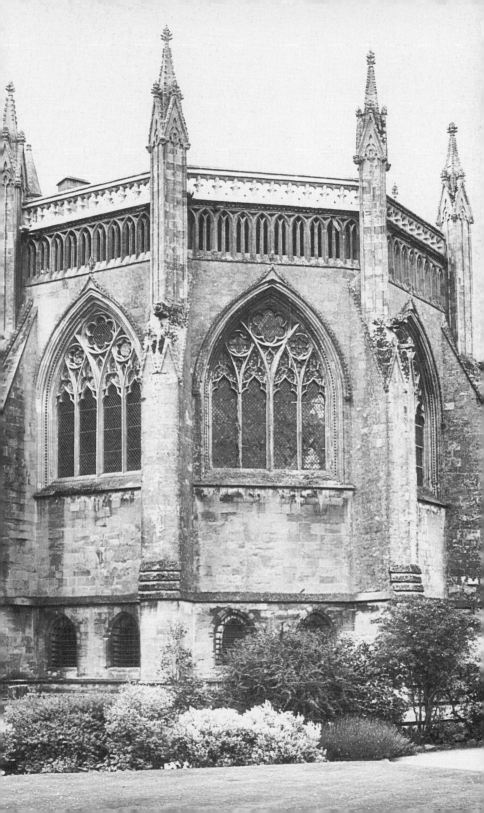

*The timbers, mainly original, of the octagonal Chapter House are supported on the stone vault with the ribs infilled with tufa, calcium carbonate formed in a stream in the Polden Hills, very light and looking like pumice-stone.*

gave the bishop their tanks on 5 February 1459/60 for the gateway built at his own expense at a cost of 500 marks (£333. 6s. 8d.), as William Worcestre noted in 1480 (see p. 158 below).

Next we come to the Chapter House, built above the treasury, now called the undercroft. The Chapter House will be examined later (pp. 151–7). The timbers inside the roof are mainly original, showing that the flat roof is as first built, as at Salisbury and Worcester, compared with the polygonal Chapter Houses at Lincoln, York and elsewhere, which have high conical roofs.

Between the Chapter House and the adjacent house there is a stone, with 'D & C' incised on one side, and what appears to be

*OPPOSITE: The porch of The Rib. The window tracery resembles that of the Chain Gate, not so far noted elsewhere. The tournament-type shields of arms are not found earlier than c.1480.*

'R.I.P.' on the other. But this does not mark the burial-place of the Dean and Chapter: the inscription actually says 'RIB'. For the adjoining house is known as The Rib, this being the last of the five (or more) 'Bishop's Ribs'. Control of the cathedral is in the hands of the dean (if present) and canons residentiary. At one time one became a resident canon simply by being collated to a canon's house. (At least two of those adjoining the present Rib were derelict, but they were still worth a canonry.) In order that the bishop might have his own supporters on the Chapter, he had in his gift a number of houses known as his Ribs, to which he could collate his chosen representatives, who thereby could become canons residentiary when vacancies occurred. All the other Ribs, of which Tower House was one, have been sold or demolished.

Elizabeth Goudge, the novelist who wrote *City of Bells* about Wells and many other books, was born in Tower House; and Canon Church, author of *Chapters in the Early History of the Church of Wells* (1894), lived at one time in what is now known as The Rib. It is recorded that a child, but not, as some say, Elizabeth Goudge, exclaimed, 'How kind it is of Mrs Church to allow the Cathedral to stand on her lawn!'

There is a path running past the east end of the cathedral for the use of the cathedral masons when working on the north side. But except when the masons are actually at work there, an iron gate prevents access to the south side of the church. This gate has to be kept shut to prevent damage by vandals. So it is now necessary to return to the West Front, to examine the south side.

### The South Side of the Cathedral

The south corner of the West Front is bonded into the outer wall of the west cloister walk, which from here onwards is built, not of ashlar like the West Front itself, but of random rubble, originally plastered over to present a surface somewhat resembling the ashlar. The porch leading into the cloister was rebuilt in 1822 using stone lying about in the Camery, and decorated over the doorway with a roof-boss presumably derived from the old Stillington chapel.

The lower part of the cloister wall, to which many excrescences were added later, dates from *c*.1230, while the upper storey is an addition of the latter half of the fifteenth century. The outer wall of the south cloister, visible from the Bishop's Green opposite the Palace Gatehouse, is in its original state, still

*The ashlar of the south-west buttress of the West Front is bonded in to the random rubble of the west cloister, which was formerly plastered to match the smooth stone of the West Front.*

71

*Looking north-west at the west cloister, recently cleaned and repaired at the expense of the Friends of Wells Cathedral.*

with the original set-offs, such as presumably topped the West Front before the towers were added.

The buildings protruding from the west side of the west cloister were to link the Choristers' House, of which a gable is visible through the wrought-iron gate in the garden between the cloister and the present Penniless Porch. The Choristers' House was built at the expense of Bishop Ralph of Shrewsbury in 1354. The Hall with its Perpendicular tracery seems small for the present number of sixteen choristers; but it must be remembered that there were until the nineteenth century only six choristers, plus, in the Middle Ages, three whose voices had just broken and who served as altarists.

The west cloister is now divided into a cathedral shop at its north end, and a restaurant in the south end. Overhead are the cathedral offices, library annexe, and choristers' practice room. When originally built they housed the choristers' practice room, the audit room of the Dean and Chapter, and the Grammar School.

Although evidently planned by Bishop Bekynton in his last

*Two stone shelters built against the east cloister walk. It is here suggested that they were for the hanging of altar-linen to dry after washing in the so-called 'Dipping-place'.*

years, this walk does not seem to have been completed till about 1480. Several of the coats-of-arms which appear on the roof-bosses are of the tournament-type shield, which does not appear elsewhere before 1479. This seems to agree with the Grammar School accounts, for no rent was paid for the Schoolhouse in College Road either in 1478–9 or 1480–1. But in the Escheator's accounts for 1490–1 it is stated that 'la Scolehows in Montre lane' (College Road) had been vacant the whole year.

The area enclosed by the cloisters, generally described as a cloister garth, was the cemetery of the canons, though since then many others have been buried there or their ashes scattered. Here it is usually called the Palm Churchyard, since it was traversed in the Palm Sunday procession (which was the principal of all processions at Wells), in the course of which priests and vicars choral tore off slips of yew and 'strawed them in the way'. This seems to have been a general practice in England, where palm trees are few and far between. It may be the reason for the general planting of yew trees in churchyards, and have nothing at all to do with long-bows. Palm Sunday was, in fact, sometimes called Yew Sunday in mediaeval Britain.

The present rather ragged yew tree may be the last survivor of three yew trees bought of Thomas Taplin, who planted them and was paid altogether 12 shillings in 1731–2.

In the same churchyard, surrounded by an iron railing, are the steps down to the stream from St Andrew's Well to the New Works (see p. 22). It may be that this, commonly known as 'the dipping place', served at one time as the baptistery of the old cathedral. Its position would correspond exactly to that of St Joseph's Well in St Joseph's Chapel at Glastonbury Abbey, and might be the reason for the positioning of the Saxon font, brought from the old cathedral, in the south transept of the present cathedral, corresponding to the relative position of the 'dipping place' to the old cathedral.

Against the east walk of the cloister are two stone shelters, which could at one time be entered from the cloister walk. No satisfactory explanation has been offered. Since it is understood that the altar-linen of the many altars was washed before the Reformation at the 'dipping-place', it may be that the washing was hung to dry on lines or wooden rods under these shelters, which would correspond to 'the place where they hang the towels to dry' in the cloisters of another cathedral. (The Latin word *tuella*, usually translated 'towel', actually means altar linen of all kinds, and especially the 'fair linen cloth'.)

At the extreme north end of the east walk, facing the churchyard, is a corbel combined with waterspout, remaining from the thirteenth-century cloister. Other thirteenth-century corbels were re-used in the fifteenth-century library above (see p. 104). The east walk was built in two halves. That is why in his will Bishop Bubwith was insistent that the library should occupy the whole length of the cloister as far as the bishop's door. At the end of the eighth bay from the north the buttress is of double width. At this same point there is a change of roof-boss. In the northern part there are armorial shields at the beginning and end of this section, with weak bosses in the intermediate bays; in the southern part are luxuriant foliage bosses, and a few pictorial bosses (a bear beating a drum, etc.). In the northern half, when the library was built on top, the thirteenth-century east wall was continued upward in ashlar over the random rubble wall below, and, being that much stronger, has only half the thickness. This is evident inside the

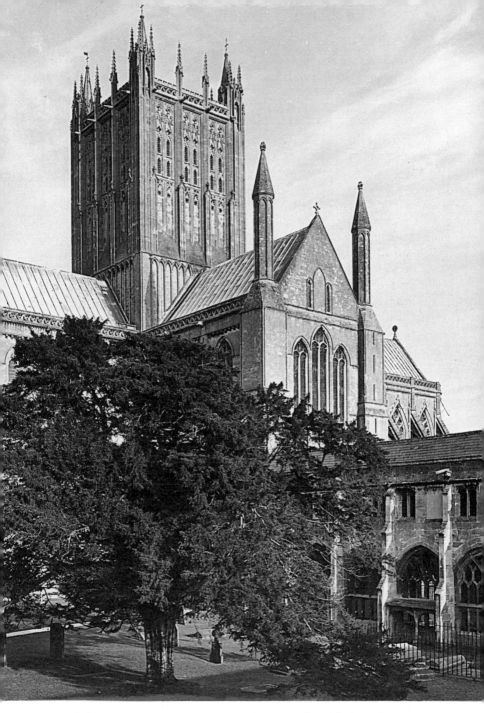

*A view of the Palm Churchyard, the east cloister walk with the Library above, and the majestic central tower.*

*Looking west along the south cloister, recently repaired and cleaned. The south wall was built in the first half of the thirteenth century, but the present cloister walk was the last part to be added to the cathedral, and finished in 1508. The upper openings were formerly glazed; the lower openings closed with wooden shutters: possibly all smashed by the Monmouth rebels awaiting trial, who were imprisoned here.*

library. In the southern half the east wall is continued upward in random rubble and keeps the same thickness throughout. On the west side it can be seen that in the southern half both the library above and the walk beneath were built together, since the relieving arch covering the last two bays of the cloister walk rises from the lower level well into the library wall above. Moreover, the same masons' marks occur both on the bottom and the upper parts.

The present south walk of the cloister, retaining the original thirteenth-century south wall intact, was built last over several years, although two bays at each end had already been completed together with the east and west walks. Most of the middle stretch, although at least one Stillington boss occurs out of sequence, was organized by Thomas Harris, the treasurer who succeeded Hugh Sugar in 1489. His initials occur on bosses in almost every bay, and documents testify to his responsibility. Work was finished in 1508, a date which appears on a boss with the initials TH in the third bay from the west, showing that work proceeded from east to west.

It should be noted that the early thirteenth-century door at the south end of the east walk has been reversed. We think of it now as an entrance to the cathedral, and it is hung accordingly. But when it was first made it was a door, normally locked, which admitted the bishop (and possibly the dean when he went visiting) to the bishop's private pleasaunce and approach to his palace.

The present double doorway giving admittance to the former Mason's Yard (and present Conservation Centre) dates from 1433, when Bishop Stafford allowed the masons' and quarriers' carts from Doulting or Street to cross his park and deliver stone to the Yard without having to go through the cloisters (see p. 161 below).

## The Camery

Halfway along the east walk there is a door opening into the Camery. Camery is a word which does not occur in the dictionary, but is said to be a secluded piece of land adjacent to a bishop's palace. One suspects that the writer of that definition had Wells in mind. The stretch of land between the old Masons' Yard and the moat is known as the Bishop's or South Camery; while the area between the old Masons' Yard and the Cathedral is technically called the Church or North Camery. The patch of grass between the Chapter House and the Rib is also technically part of the Camery and so appears in old leases, for there were at least two cottages or buildings in this area.

The Camery is today once again laid out as a garden, including a herb garden. At one time when it was let out, it nurtured mainly fruit and vegetables. The Dean and Chapter resumed ownership and occupation of it in the nineteenth century.

Now just inside the Camery, as one enters from the cloister, there is a colourful and lucid plan and explanation of the excavations carried out here in 1894 and again in 1978–80, which revealed the foundations of successive early chapels, which together formed the east end of the previous cathedral. The foundations now exposed are those of the Lady Chapel by the cloister as rebuilt at the charges of Robert Stillington, Bishop of Bath and Wells 1465–91, who never visited it during

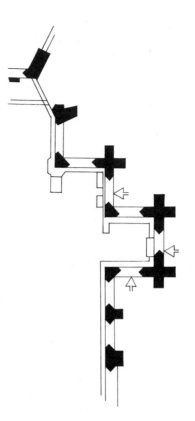

*Plan showing the position of three obvious breaks in the building of the eastward extension below window-level, c.1320–1330.*

his lifetime, but was buried here at his death. It will be seen that its length equalled that of the cathedral transept as well as most of the cathedral quire. The panelling of its west wall survives on the east wall of the cloister. When the whole building was similarly panelled, and still had its fan-vaulting (of which several bosses survive and are displayed in the cloister walks), it must have been a sumptuous sight, and very similar to Sherborne Abbey church.

On the south wall of the south transept can be seen the same sort of blind arcading of lancets as outside the north transept, but here it seems to have been still more altered and adapted, and was obviously meant to be hidden from view by the successive Lady Chapels. At the south-east corner of the transept can be seen the water-table of the early vestry opening from St Martin's chapel, identical with the vestry on the north side, where its place was taken by the Chapter House steps. Above this is the blocked doorway formerly leading across a small bridge from the stairs to the transept of Stillington's Lady Chapel.

The second buttress of the south quire aisle (counting from the transept) is of double thickness, because this was opposite the east wall of the quire of c.1180, before the eastern arm was extended towards the eastern Lady Chapel. The bay immediately beyond this was an ambulatory of the same height and perhaps width as the quire aisle.

In each of the following bays, of the west and south walls of St Katherine's chapel, and the south wall of St John Baptist's chapel, there are very pronounced breaks in the bonding of the masonry below aisle or chapel window level. These breaks give firm proof that the extension of the quire took place from west to east to meet the completed Lady Chapel. They also lead to the supposition that there was a break of two, three or more years at various stages in the progress of this extension. Possibly this was due to the sinking of the foundations in waterlogged soil. If this is so, the delay in completion must have been even greater. It is known that the foundations of St Katherine's chapel go down at least 11 feet (3.4 m), whereas at the south transept wall and the Chapter House they are only 4 feet 6 inches (1.37 m) deep. No matter what caused the delay, it does indicate that since St Katherine's chapel was completed by 21 September 1329 when Bishop Drokensford was buried there and arrangements were made for his and other obits to be celebrated there, work on the extension of the thirteenth-century quire can hardly have begun later than about 1320 (see p. 19 above).

Two designs were used alternately for the windows of the quire aisles, but on this south side they have got out of order. This must be due to a mistake when they were put in, not noticed until too late.

The double corner-buttresses set diagonally on St Katherine's and St John's chapels have already been mentioned (p. 52) as the possible inspiration of William Wynford's use of the same feature both on his south-west tower and his work elsewhere. All these buttresses, including those cutting the parapet all round the high roof of the quire, were surmounted not by spirelets but by castellated caps. These can be seen to advantage on the flying buttress built at ground level at the south-east corner of the Lady Chapel (where the iron gate is) to

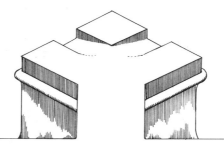

*Diagram of castellated caps of the buttresses on the presbytery extension, c.1335–40.*

act as a tell-tale in case of that corner of the chapel sinking into the water. This flier has a reversed arch underground which will give visible warning of trouble above in the event of subterranean upheaval.

Just before reaching the iron gate, the site of the mediaeval vestry adjoining the south wall of the Lady Chapel can be seen. This was demolished by order of the Dean and Chapter in June 1822, but the Master of the Fabric (Canon Frankland) observed afterwards:

> 'If the Master of the Fabrick had known that the little building in the garden on the South Side of the Cathedral was co-eval with the Lady's Chapel, and was built (as it proved to be) into the very walls of the main fabrick, he would not have consented to its removal.—The destruction of it was very difficult in execution; and so expensive that it can hardly be repaid by the expected healthiness of the inner wall.'

*OPPOSITE: The east end of the enlarged cathedral is very near the wells, which flood from time and time. In the later fourteenth century this delicate flying buttress was added, with an inverted arch underneath, to serve as a tell-tale if disaster threatened the foundations.*

## Chapter Three

# INSIDE THE
# CATHEDRAL

*The Nave*

MOST PEOPLE nowadays enter the cathedral through the small south-west door, although the main entrance is by the magnificent North Porch. It is said that the laity entered by a doorway, now blocked, leading into the west cloister and then by the door under the south-west tower, through the area now occupied by the cathedral shop. But there are very few mentions of any lay people entering the cathedral in the Middle Ages. The cathedral community was offering worship and prayer for a large part of each day (and night) on behalf of all the people in the diocese. Unlike a parish church where all the people present offer their worship, praise and prayers as best they can, in a cathedral the praise and worship and prayer are offered by the clergy in as superb a way as possible on behalf of all the people who are not there, being engaged upon their normal avocations.

That still applies to some of the weekday services, when there are sometimes no more than a dozen lay people present. Worship is still being offered on behalf of all the folk in Somerset and South Avon, whether residents or visitors on holiday. On nearly every Saturday in summer there are also special services in the nave arranged at the request of various organizations from all over Somerset and South Avon. One can safely say that the cathedral is now used far more than ever

*OPPOSITE: The nave. Note how the uninterrupted series of arches in the triforium emphasizes the horizontal ('sold-on-the-ground') aspect, and also carries the eye quickly forward from west to east.*

before. Now on many occasions the nave is packed to capacity with worshippers. In the Middle Ages it was used only for processions on saints' days and other festivals. Marked on the floor of the nave in the second, third and fourth bays from the west until the early nineteenth century were circles, eleven on each side, to show the positions to be taken by the clergy in procession, at the Station there, where a Collect was said before the procession resumed its movement up the nave and back to the quire. So far as the present century goes, the attendance at Holy Communion (the only attendances that are recorded) was 5,391 in 1903; in 1983 it was 19,269.

In the nave the Doulting stone (see p. 30 above) is seen at its best. It has a warm, cream tone, here seen in its natural state, unwashed or otherwise cleaned. The design of the nave is simple, but extra warmth is given by the luxurious carving at all levels.

The proportions are simple, inasmuch as each bay of the aisles is a perfect square. (The dimensions, and their metric equivalents, are listed on p. 184.) The measurement right across the nave from stone bench on one side to stone bench on the other, i.e. the place you actually touch when you start building, is exactly 66 feet or 22 yards, one cricket pitch, using the old practical measure of one chain, which was literally a chain. The chain was also used to measure the height of the underside of the vault-rib at ridge level (again, the place you touch from scaffolding). From there to the floor is exactly one chain: 22 yards: 66 feet. From the ground to the capital of the respond, where the vault starts its curve, is 44 feet; the vertical distance from there to the ridge, 22 feet; that is, two-thirds and one-third.

The shortest distance between opposite pillars of the nave, i.e. from the projecting shaft on one side to the equivalent shaft on the opposite side (the place you touch with string or measuring-tape) exactly equals the distance from the same projecting shaft to the equivalent shaft on the pillar next-but-one on the same side; and so on. Each measurement is adhered to with great accuracy.

In France, and on the Continent generally, the responds of the vault, i.e. wall-shafts from which the vault springs, usually rise from the floor; in England usually from the capitals of the main arcade. Wells and Salisbury (which owes much to Wells

*OPPOSITE: The impressive compound pillars of the nave, as seen from the south aisle. They maintain the same design as those built c.1180 in the quire.*

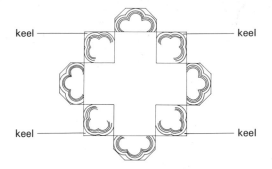

*Plan of pillars in main arcades, c.1180–1225.*

in its design) are the only cathedrals where the responds rise from above the triforium openings. In Wells uniquely the triforium consists of an unbroken row of arches extending all the way from west to east, so that the eye is carried eastwards all the time. The triforium therefore presents a very strong horizontal emphasis, such as we have already seen on the West Front. The French emphasize verticality. In England we like a building both to be, and to appear to be, solid on the ground.

In 1931 Sir Harold Brakspear drew attention to special features of Gothic design which appeared in churches and cathedrals in the western part of England, and especially along the Welsh border, and which seemed different from the Gothic style as it appears in France and the more easterly parts of Britain more strongly influenced by French style. For instance, minor but clear examples are apparent in the triforium where capitals are wholly absent: the mouldings run 'up and over' without a break; similar arches of identical width are inside taller ones, leaving a space in the tympanum for a small carving.

Wells has been called the earliest completely Gothic building in Europe because it is the first time the compound pillar, consisting of a multiplicity of shafts, is used throughout the building. (The pillar design in the nave is the same as that first used in the quire, *c*.1180.) All other buildings of *c*.1180 have circular Romanesque drums for their pillars, or alternate rounds and squares. The Wells pillars look complicated at first, but on close examination they are seen to consist of a square cross with three shafts in each corner, and three shafts on the end of each bar of the cross. Each corner shaft is keeled: the others are not. This gives the design vitality: if all shafts were keeled, they would look fussy and restless.

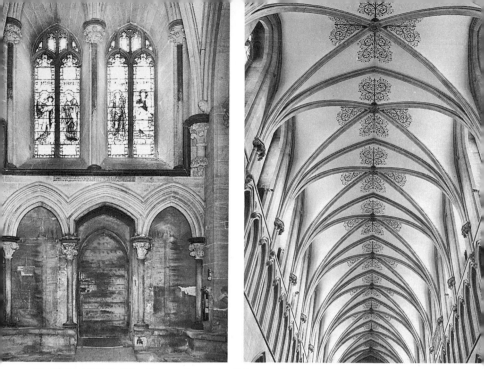

ABOVE LEFT: *The flattened arches of the small west doors are carried on short vertical stilts, an idea copied at Wells from the doors of the old transept vestries—the south one now blocked, the north one still in use for the Chapter House steps. This design was followed at Salisbury and then at Westminster.*

ABOVE RIGHT: *The nave vault, originally painted in the first half of the thirteenth century; repainted in 1844 with each bay identical; and the vault repaired and repainted following the scheme of 1844 in 1985.*

It has been said that the Wells design is more Norman (or Romanesque) than Gothic, because of the thickness of the walls. But the houses in Vicars' Close, built after 1360 in the Perpendicular style, consisting originally of one single room upstairs and one downstairs, with interior measurements of 13 by 20 feet (3.9 × 6m), have walls which are 3 feet (1m) thick.

The small west doors at the ends of the aisles have flattened arches on vertical springers. These can hardly be later than c.1230. The great west door also has a flattened arch on vertical springers, as also the door from the north quire aisle into the undercroft passage, but these are less noticeable. They all appear to derive from the flattened arches above the moulded shafts without capitals which occur in the doors of the old vestries, in the north transept, east aisle (now leading to the Chapter House steps), and the south transept, in St Martin's chapel, now blocked. These two doors seem to belong to the original build of c.1190. Flattened arches on vertical springers are later found at Salisbury, and later still, at Westminster.

Painted patterns were discovered on the vault of the nave when whitewash, daubed over everything after the Reformation, was removed in 1844. New painted decoration, based on the pattern discovered on the vault of the second bay from the west, was then repeated on each bay of the nave, and a simpler version in the transepts. Much plaster was renewed at that time, but was put on too wet, and cracked later. Dust then accumulated in the hairlines and made them appear from the ground far worse then they actually were. In 1984–5 the limewash and paint were removed, the plaster repaired where necessary, and limewash and paint renewed, following exactly the same scheme as in 1844. In the course of removing the former decoration it was discovered, as was to be expected, that the original pattern had been different in each bay. This is what happens in all the sculptured roundels and tympana at triforium level in the cathedral, as well as on the West Front. While all decoration appears at first glance regular and similar, each design is seen on closer inspection to be different. In the case of the decoration of the vault this was not discovered for certain until the work of renewal was almost completed in 1985.

No mention has been made so far of the most striking feature of the nave: the scissor-arches at the east end. The omission is deliberate. These will be dealt with when we reach the crossing and transepts (pp. 111–114 below). But it is reasonable to speak now of the Rood on the arch facing the nave. Similar figures were placed there in the fifteenth century by the treasurer, Hugh Sugar. Those may have been replacements of earlier figures. They were destroyed at the Reformation, but the stump of the wooden cross remained, fixed with lead in its stone socket, until 1920, when a new cross was placed here experimentally by order of Dean Armitage Robinson. That was a plain cross which did not seem to fit in well with the surrounding architecture. Sir Charles Nicholson, the architect, designed a new, more decorative one; figures of Christ, Mary his mother, and John, 'the beloved disciple', were carved by G Tosi of Brompton; and the whole paid for by Mrs Jessie Head, the sister of Douglas Maclean, who is commemorated in a window in Corpus Christi chapel.

In the clerestory on the south side of the nave there is a

*Two large corbel-heads of a king and a bishop in spandrels of the nave arcade. These supported the timber brackets of an organ built out from the triforium in 1310.*

tomb–like parapet of *c*.1450, enclosing the wall-passage in the fifth bay from the crossing (sixth from west). This has been described as a minstrel's gallery, but there is very little space there for performers or their instruments. In Rouen there remains the text, with music and stage directions, of a nativity play regularly performed there. During the singing of the *Te Deum* some boys or youths, dressed as shepherds with staffs, take up their position below, while one chorister dressed as an angel, wearing amice and alb, standing in a high place, announced:

> 'Fear not: for behold I give you good tidings of great joy. For unto you is born this day in the city of David a Saviour, which is Christ the Lord.'

He is joined by two other choristers on each side, and all together 'in the vaults of the church' begin singing:

> 'Glory to God in the highest, and on earth peace.'

Similar plays exist, mostly in fragmentary form elsewhere. This gallery in Wells Cathedral would provide the ideal setting for the chorister angels.

In the seventh bay from the crossing, in the spandrels of the main arcade are two corbels, one in the form of a king's head, the other of a bishop, representing, as usual, the civil and spiritual life. The carving has been identified as belonging stylistically to the early fourteenth century. The tops of the corbels are absolutely flat, showing that the squared ends of timbers rested on them. These corbels were almost certainly to support a wooden gallery built out from the triforium to support the organ, used to play briefly between the verses of plainsong hymns, sung unaccompanied in procession, to make sure the singers start the next verse on the right note. (This is the position of the present organ at Strasbourg, but on the north side; the organ at Chartres is in this position on the south, but two bays further east, since Chartres has a short nave.) Of the organ itself we know that on 28 May 1310 the Dean and Chapter allocated some of the oak tree at Winscombe, 12 miles (19 km) away, to the building of the organ, although the Dean had already assigned the whole tree for some other purpose.

Later, when the present pulpitum had been built, the organ—very much smaller then—was moved to the position of the present one.

### The Windows

Small specimens of fifteenth-century stained glass remain in some of the tracery lights. The windows, very wide lancets in proportion to their height at that period, were filled with identical Perpendicular tracery at the end of the fourteenth century. On the south side four windows have been filled with stained glass by C E Kempe between 1897 and 1904. His scheme for filling all eight windows on that side survives in the cathedral library. Almost certainly there was no glass at all in these windows until the fifteenth century. Even 'white' glass was far too expensive. Probably the lower lights had oiled linen, which admitted a certain amount of light, and kept out a certain amount of wind and rain; while in the clerestory were wooden shutters, which could be opened or shut as required by a man running along the passage there. The windows over the small west doors were put in by Powell & Co. of Whitefriars in the 1890s.

The great west window consisting of three large lancets had to withstand the full force of Atlantic gales. Also damage to the glass has been heard and seen to occur due to birds, unable to stop, ramming into it and splintering it with their beaks.

Bishop Harewell (1366–86) gave 100 marks (£66. 13s. 4d.) for a new west window, a terrific price in those days. It was all reglazed by Robert Creyghtone [I], Dean 1660–70, and Bishop 1670–2, at a cost of £140. The two side lights, much patched since, survive from his gift. There is not very much stained glass, apart from heraldic arms, of this period in Britain, and it would be interesting to know who the artist was in this case. The figures of Moses and Elijah at the top show that the subject was the Transfiguration of Christ. Beneath these figures are, on the south side King Ine, legendary founder of this church, who is very reminiscent here of a playing-card; and, on the north, the rather stout Bishop Ralph of Shrewsbury, unlike the effigy on his tomb, who built Vicars' Close, the Choristers' House, and was responsible for the digging of the Palace Moat, and also for the efficient working of the church in Somerset during the Black Death (pages 20–1 above).

The window suffered badly in the great storm of 1703, when the Eddystone lighthouse was blown down, and the bishop, Richard Kidder, and his wife were killed by the fall of a chimney in the Palace. By 1813 the state of the centre light was so bad that it was removed, and the space filled with second-hand glass from Rouen, bought from English dealers who had acquired it during the Treaty of Amiens, 1802. This was most unsuitable for that position. The coloured scheme of arrangement, drawn by W R Eginton, survives in the cathedral library. But the constituent panels are among the most interesting glass in the cathedral. The glass was removed from this light in 1926, and the various panels used to fill it were disposed in various places about the cathedral, where they will be discussed in due course. A new centre light was made by A K

Nicholson, using coloured enamels on white glass very largely, like the seventeenth-century glazier. From a distance this centre light matches the side lights very well. But again the wind caused trouble. Although this new light was inserted only in 1931, the metal bars holding the glass in position had to be almost doubled eight years later.

In the latter part of the fourteenth century the stone mullions of this window, facing into the nave, had to be completely renewed, together with the parapet of the west gallery under the window. One can guess that originally there were round shafts of blue lias rising from the round shafts of Doulting stone issuing from the sloping west wall. These lias shafts would be face-bedded, and easily split at the best of times. So they had to be replaced with Doulting, but the round blue lias bases and caps remain. Beneath this gallery with its Perpendicular parapet designed by William Wynford, runs another passage within the thickness of the wall, behind the sloping face just mentioned. It is this passage which has the holes for vicars choral and choristers to sing through on major festivals, their voices amplified by reflection from the back wall (see p. 39 above).

At ground level there are four large shafts of Draycott conglomerate. When polished this is sometimes called Wonderstone. We do not know if they date from the thirteenth century: one certainly is a modern replacement. There are five monumental floorslabs of the same stone dated between 1644 and 1655 about the cathedral. The same stone in rubble form was used to build the Archdeaconry, and occurs also in the outer walls of the cloisters, and of Vicars' Close.

The chapel under the north-west tower was dedicated to Holy Cross. It was later and until recently used as the bishop's consistory court; and earlier this century as the choristers' vestry.

Hanging over the entrance to this space is the late thirteenth-century wooden pyx-canopy, designed to hold the pyx containing the elements consecrated at Mass. Formerly it was kept

*OPPOSITE: The great west window. The north and south lights date from c.1670, having been inserted at the expense of Robert Creyghtone [I], Dean of Wells 1660–70, Bishop of Bath and Wells 1670–72. The centre light, also inserted at the same time, had to be renewed with Continental glass in 1813. The present centre light designed by A K Nicholson was put in in 1931.*

93

in the undercroft, and then in the library. It is cylindrical, nearly four feet (1.22 m) high, with an internal diameter of 14½ inches (37 cm). It is made of oak, but has at some period been repaired with deal. Traces of red and white paint remain. Pyx-canopies, later in date, survive at Milton Abbey, Tewkesbury and Dennington (Suffolk).

## 'The Break'

At a certain point in the building of the nave work was completely suspended. This is generally called 'the break'. When work was resumed after the break there were a number of small changes in design and workmanship. This was almost certainly due to the Interdict, since the presumed dating of this part of the building coincides so nearly with the known dates of the Interdict (see p. 12 above).

Those who are interested in identifying these differences should stand in the south aisle in the fourth bay from the west end, where it is easier to see than on the north side. Examination of the south wall will show that at a certain point near the right hand wall-shaft smallish stones (one handspan high) give way to big stones. The line of this change from small to bigger stones moves eastward as it rises, because it would be impossible to cut off a building with a sheer vertical end. So larger stones are seen both above slightly to the left, and also to the right at lower levels. This implies that there was a certain amount of mechanization after 1213, by means of a new big wheel or crane to raise and swing the larger stones into position, which would be too heavy for one man.

If you now turn round, facing the north side of the nave, and look at the roundels carved in the spandrels of the triforium arcade, you will see that towards the east these carvings are all countersunk in their roundels; while to the west the carvings in the roundels are flush with the ashlar surface.

Now look a bit lower at the hood-moulds of the main arcade. Towards the east they terminate in small carved heads. But towards the west there are no head-stops: the hood-moulds meet at points in mitre-joints.

Look now at the capital of the nave pillar nearest to you on your right side (i.e. east). You will see that the carving of the stiff-leaf foliage of this capital is quite simple. Compare that with the carvings on the capitals to your left (westwards). Here the foliage is quite luxuriant and deeply undercut.

Finally, look at the base of the pillar on the eastward side.

The diagonal tool-marks are quite clearly visible. The mason has held his chisel and struck it diagonally, as still today, for ease of cutting. Or he may have still been using a stone-axe and likewise striking the stone diagonally. Compare this with the base of the pillar on the west side. Here the stone has been cut in precisely the same way, but the foreman has told the mason to tidy it up afterwards by going over the tool-marks vertically with a comb or toothed drag, so as to leave small vertical lines obliterating the diagonal tool-marks. These are five easily recognizable means of distinguishing work done before 1209 from work resumed after 1213—probably not until Henry III's reign (i.e. from late 1216 onwards).

Coinciding with these changes in the masonry, there is a change also in the jointing of the roof timbers, where before 1209 we find the ordinary notched lap-joint, but after 1213 the secret-notch lap-joint.

### The Nave Capitals

While moving up the nave we may note various carved capitals which are of special interest. The third free-standing pillar from the west on the south side has a male head emerging from a sheath-like scallop. A female head appearing from a similar sheath is on the second pillar on the north side. This pillar on the north side also has a double-bodied lion with a single head; and dragons with leafy tails.

The third pillar on the north has two doves, and two birds with dragons' heads and leafy tails. The fourth pillar on the north has a fine goat's head, with long sweeping horns; a ram's head with stubby curly horns; two birds eating from the foliage, with a grotesque head between them; and two birds preening themselves. The fifth pillar, north side, has two beasts facing and snarling at each other; and two birdlike dragons, one wearing a coronet, their tails sprouting leaves.

The corresponding pillar on the south side, fifth from west, shows two dragons fighting: one thrusts a spear down the throat of the other, which backs away in pain with wings spread; also two small devil-heads on long necks, and one large devil-head, all with asses' ears.

The seventh pillar on the south has two birds with long twisted necks and human heads, one wearing a jester's cap. In the re-entrant angles you can easily see that the ends of the foliage have been cut off to form a loose mitre-joint, which is proof that the capitals were carved in the lodge or elsewhere, probably indoors during the winter, and were then cut to fit and inserted when spring came. The eighth pillar on the south, adjoining the pulpit and chantry, shows a man being attacked by a lion, now headless; a lyre bird, and a now headless eagle.

Back to the north side, to the sixth pillar from the west, on the east side of the north door. Here is the smiling lion. As you enter by the north door and look up, you see the lion smiling at you. When you pass him later, on leaving the cathedral, and look at him, you will see he has a rather severe expression. But if before you go, you put a donation in the money-box there and look back at him, you will see him smiling once more. (The official version describes the lion as licking himself like a cat.)

On the seventh pillar on the north side, adjoining the chantry, a fox is carrying off a goose, watched in dismay by the farmer carrying a club and stone; there are also three birds preening themselves and feeding from the foliage. Inside the chantry are a spoonbill swallowing a frog; and a devil with a long curly tail holding a fish in one hand and a billhook in the other.

On the next pillar, at the east end of the chantry is a corpse-like figure leering, and a fine figure of a packman carrying his wares. Opposite him, on the north wall, is a pedlar or pilgrim carrying his kit on a stick over his shoulder, and holding a curious cylindrical object. The wall-shaft next along on the north wall at the corner of the transept has a freak or devil's head, and one of the best tooth-ache capitals. With a torch and a step-ladder it is possible to see right inside his mouth, where his tongue presses on the aching tooth. (This seems to prove that the so-called 'tooth-ache' capitals really do picture tooth-ache and not trigeminal neuralgia as the doctors try to make out.)

These last two capitals are outside the virgers' office, situated in the west aisle of the north transept, used at one time as the library, and then as the subdean's court. This room contains the boards decorated with Tudor painting which conceal parts of the clock. The dean also had a court, but its position is at present unknown.

The last pillar on the south side has a capital with two men's heads facing south-west, one with curly hair and the other wearing a cowl, with his tongue out. Was he another tooth-ache sufferer? On the other side, facing south-east into the transept, a man with tooth-ache bears a scroll with his name

*ABOVE LEFT: One of the eleven 'tooth-ache' carvings. This one, near the Virgers' office, actually has his tongue on the aching tooth.*

*ABOVE RIGHT: Alabaster carving of the Ascension in the Bubwith Chantry. The seventeenth-century frame is Dutch or Flemish.*

ELIAS P., i.e. Elijah the Prophet; and next to him a man who is completely bald, perhaps meant to portray Elisha. ('Go up, thou bald head.' *2 Ki.* $2^{23}$.)

### The Chantry Chapels

At the east end of the nave are two hexagonal chantry chapels, both the same height and shape, but otherwise very different. From a distance, however, they appear quite symmetrical. The one on the north side of the nave is dedicated to Holy Cross, and the altar to St Saviour. This is where Nicholas Bubwith, Bishop 1407–24, was buried. His chapel was already finished when he made his will in October, 1424. On a corbel on the west wall of the chapel is the earliest existing representation of the arms of the See, impaling Bubwith. Here also is an alabaster panel of the Ascension, with the eleven Apostles and the Virgin Mary looking on while all but the feet of Christ is concealed by a curtain–like cloud. This is the customary representation, presumably derived from the dramatic performance on a raised staging or cart. So also, held up like a stage property, is a board or slab with the distinct marks of Christ's feet, to represent the rocky outcrop with barely-recognizable indentations still shown to visitors today in the Chapel of the Ascension on the Mount of Olives. Unusual are the two angels, one with remarkable breath-control blowing a trumpet as he flies, the other beating out some complicated rhythm with crossed hands on the kettledrums slung over his neck. The alabaster is English of the fifteenth century; the frame Dutch of the seventeenth. The figures over the altar were a gift from priests and others in the diocese who are associated with the shrine of Our Lady at Walsingham.

The chapel on the south side was built with a bequest from Hugh Sugar, canon residentiary, treasurer of the cathedral and Bishop Stillington's Vicar general. He died in April, 1489, so work cannot have begun on the chapel until after his will was proved on 5 May 1489. The chapel is dedicated to St Edmund of Abingdon, who was Archbishop of Canterbury 1233–40. Inside the chantry in the corner high up over the entrance to the pulpit is a solitary owl (difficult to see without a torch); in the opposite corner a man declaiming with gown and scroll.

Built out from the north-west corner of this chapel is the pulpit and tomb of William Knight, Bishop 1541–7, in pronounced Renaissance style. The inscription under the cornice of the pulpit reads: PREACHE · THOV · THE · WORDE · BE · FER-VENT · IN · SEASON · AND · OVT · OF · SEASON · IMPROVE · REBVKE · EXHORTE · W̄ · ALL · LONGE · SVFFERYNG · & · DOCTRYNE · 2 TIMO. This corresponds word for word with the text (2 Tim. $4^2$) as it appears in Coverdale's Great Bible of 1539. The second edition of 1540 has some differences. There are, however, some minor abbreviations: WYTH is contracted to W̄ , SVFFERYNGE loses its final E, and AND is contracted. All these small changes were made by reason of lack of space on the pulpit. When the Authorised Version of the English Bible appeared in 1611 IMPROVE was altered to REPROVE, in order to conform to the new translation; but other more difficult changes were not made. Until the end of the eighteenth century there was a wooden tester or sounding-board over the pulpit. This was painted apple-green with Bishop Knight's coat-of-arms in the middle and the text in black-letter QVI EX DEO EST VERBA DEI AVDIT: 'He that is of God heareth God's words' (John $8^{47}$). So the preacher, to whom the first text refers, was addressed in

*The nave pulpit, built by William Knight, bishop 1541–47, as his tomb.*

English in Roman letters, but the congregation was expected to read Latin and in black-letter. The bishop is buried beneath his pulpit.

On the floor below, due west of the pulpit, is the blue lias slab with the indents of a brass of a priest, with a long inscription below, four heraldic shields, and another inscription round the edge of the slab, with roundels at each corner, which presumably held the emblems of the Four Evangelists. Legend, backed by several eighteenth-century writers, says that this covered the grave of John Free (in Greek, Phreas) who had been provided by the Pope to the see of Bath and Wells on the death of Bekynton, and had been duly elected by the Chapter. But within a month, and before his consecration, he had died of food poisoning at the age of 35.

Nearly all the indents had been deprived of their brasses immediately after the act abolishing chantries in 1547, when they, and anything else removeable, had been taken up and sold by the Dean and Chapter, in order to provide money for the essential renewal of the lead roof. So the slab next to Free's also lost its effigy, and two hundred years later William Broderib, the organist, used the same slab, by having his own name carved on it, to cover his own coffin. The worst loss in this respect is the removal of the huge brass measuring 9 feet by 2 ft 4 in (2.74 × 0.71 m) and subsidiary brasses on the enormous indent measuring 15 ft 1 in by 6 ft 4 in (4.60 × 1.93 m.) of Walter Haselshaw, Dean 1295–1302 and Bishop 1302–6, which lies immediately on the south side of Bubwith's chantry, which partially covers it. What looks like a square mousehole at the bottom south-west corner of the chantry was made by order of Dean Armitage Robinson to see if the chantry had actually been built over some of the brass letters. He there found a letter E, which he removed, but it has now vanished without a trace.

### The Crossing and Transepts

In the wall of the easternmost bay of the south aisle of the nave there is a change of stone. A much rougher, pock-marked pebbly stone is used instead of the much smoother Doulting. As has been already mentioned, the Doulting quarry belonged to Glastonbury Abbey. At the pillar dividing St Martin's chapel from St Calixtus' on the east side of the south transept this new pebbly, pock-marked stone, known as Chilcote Conglomerate, was introduced. Apart from the cathedral it occurs in Wells at this period only in the Canons' Barn (now part of the Cathedral School), which was built before 1191. In 1184 the old Glastonbury Abbey was burnt down. Rebuilding began almost at once. It seems likely that the abbot required exclusive use of his quarry at Doulting until the most important buildings were rebuilt. So the Dean and Chapter had to make use of this Chilcote Conglomerate, which came from the Dean and Chapter's own land about $2\frac{1}{2}$ miles (4 km) from Wells. The distance was much less than the distance from Doulting, and the conglomerate was much harder (but correspondingly harder to work), and did not have to be properly bedded. Being both rough and hard, it was not suitable for carving. Fortunately, there was a certain amount of Doulting stone stock-piled at Wells; so while the Chilcote was used almost exclusively in the upper parts of the transepts, and almost all the transept exterior, Doulting could still be used for the carved work and for much of the interior ground-level ashlar.

In most churches in the Middle Ages the stone was covered with plaster, which was then painted. If the paint was not pictorial, red lines were usually ruled and painted over the whitewashed surface in imitation of 'bricks', the red lines taking the place, approximately, of the white mortar. One would expect that the pock-marked Chilcote Conglomerate would have provided a fine 'key' for the plaster. The fact that the use of the Chilcote was abandoned as soon as Doulting stone was available again, albeit from somebody else's quarry at three times the distance, proves that the ashlar was not plastered at Wells. In fact, the mediaeval decorative scheme now survives only in the lantern over the crossing, now hidden above the fan-vault, and is discernible there only with strong artificial lighting. The ashlar was covered with ochre wash, very much the same colour as the natural stone. On this lines were drawn freehand in the lantern, but would almost certainly have been ruled at ground-level, with white lines resembling white mortar. The surviving lines in the lantern are not superimposed exactly on the lines of the rough mortar, but generally run on the smoother ashlar parallel to the actual mortar-lines. When work was resumed on the tower in 1313 no more colouring was used. So there is a sudden change from the ochre with white lines to bare ashlar stone and mortar at the point where the work of raising the tower was resumed. Yet this is wholly unnoticeable except with the powerful artificial light already mentioned. The change would have been completely invisible when viewed from the ground, as must have been possible right up to c.1480, when the fan-vault was inserted over the crossing.

Did not this crossing-vault, smart as it is, mean the loss of a striking view up the lantern? This would be especially true when the lancets of the lantern were filled with glass, before the windows were blocked and other alterations made (see p. 64 above) as a result of the fire of c.1439. In the year or years immediately preceding 1480 four cathedrals or major churches vaulted their crossings and closed off their lanterns. I think this must be because in those days, when there was no artificial heating, the warmth from the bodies of canons, choristers and vicars choral, together with the hot air expelled by so many singing voices, would rise to the top of the lantern. There it would be instantly cooled by the cold window-glass, and descend in a rush upon the tonsured heads of the occupants of the quire, and make the pages of such service-books as there were to flutter over, causing everyone to lose his place. The cure, once the cause was understood, was to block off the lantern, so as to have roofs of a single continuous height running the whole length of the building. The draught was thereby eliminated.

In the south transept the capitals on the west side are the most interesting in the cathedral. The first free-standing pillar south of the crossing has carvings of an old lady taking a thorn out of her foot; a sufferer from tooth-ache; and (west side) a cobbler mending shoes. We have already met some carvings of tooth-ache in the east end of the nave aisles. In fact, there are eleven tooth-ache carvings at Wells. One French cathedral has five tooth-aches, but eleven seems to be the record. They have sometimes been wrongly associated with William Bytton II (Bishop 1267–74), who was credited with miraculous powers, both before and after his death, of curing tooth-ache. He had not been born when these capitals were carved. The explanation seems simple. Carvers on either side of their bench were chipping away at their capitals. One day one had tooth-ache, so his unsympathetic mate on the other side of the bench made fun of him by carving a face tormented by tooth-ache. The others all laughed, and all, with the exception of the sufferer, then made their own toothache carvings. Some of those

*The Cathedral Library over the east cloister was built in two stages between 1425 and 1433. The present shelves, desks and benches date from 1686.*

dissatisfied with their first attempt, including, we presume, the Elias-carver (see p. 96 above), made another. Alternatively, this whole exercise may have been an experiment in cure by homoeopathy.

The capital on the next pillar southward is the most famous of all, since it tells a story in four 'chapters' in an anti-clockwise direction. The story begins in the south-east corner of the capital. While a boy, wearing what looks like a balaclava helmet, holds a basket full of fruit (grapes or cider-apples), an old man grasps a bunch of fruit; he prepares to cut it off with the sickle in his right hand. Before doing so, he wisely looks over his shoulder to see if anyone is watching . . .

Move to the right-hand (north-east) corner. Somebody *was* watching. This man, holding an axe in his left hand, points with the large index-finger of his right hand, and says: 'Somebody is stealing your fruit!' He is talking to a farmer with a large hat, tied under his chin, and holding a pitch-fork, carved out of stone, c.1190.

Move to the north-west corner. The boy has run away. The farmer has caught the thief by his right ear (or long hair), and prepares to hit him over the head with his pitch-fork. In the last scene he does so, and his hat falls off.

This capital has no didactic purpose. The master mason had told the carver to make so many capitals $20\frac{1}{2}$ inches (52 cm) high by such and such a day. The carver having carved nothing but foliage capitals ever since 1180 (or whenever the present cathedral was begun), was tired of carving leaves and wanted a change of subject. The master mason was not concerned about the subject, only about the measurements. He found the finished capital was exactly $20\frac{1}{2}$ inches (52 cm) high, and ordered it to be set on the pillar. Because people liked it, we now have all the other figure and animal carvings in the nave.

The door nearest this pillar leads to the cathedral library, built over the east cloister, 1425–33, incorporating eleven thirteenth-century heads from the earlier cloister (p. 74 above). It is said to have been the largest mediaeval library building in England, with an internal length of 162 feet (50.4 m). The library itself, because of the value of many of the books and the very meagre part-time voluntary staff, cannot be opened to the general public, but can be used by those doing genuine research, who must get permission in writing well in advance. On the other hand, in order to show the public a selection of the interesting books and documents, an exhibition, changed

*This Aldine edition of Aristotle, printed at Venice 1495–98, belonged to Erasmus. It was given to the Cathedral Library by William Turner, Dean of Wells 1551–54 and 1560–68. The notes in the margin were made by Erasmus.*

every year, is open in the ante-room of the library during the summer months (from Easter Monday until the end of September) on Monday, Tuesday, Wednesday and Thursday afternoons between 2.30 and 4 p.m. Fridays and Saturdays are kept free for research and cleaning only.

The next door to the east leads to the former Escheator's office, where the cleaners now keep their materials. This minute room was at one time used as the choristers' vestry. But there were only six choristers then.

In the south wall is the fine tomb of Bishop William of March (de Marchia) (see p. 19 above), with some magnificently carved heads and figures of angels sadly damaged. Much original paint remains, and a series of painted heads may be discerned along the string-course or cornice alongside by the door leading to the Escheator's office, just mentioned.

The reredos adjoining it may have belonged to a chantry chapel of de Marchia, being formerly at right angles to its present position. It looks more recent than the tomb itself. It has also been suggested that it stood against the pulpitum, north of the entrance to the quire; and that the present brass of *c*.1810, being a copy of an earlier one, actually belonged to that reredos, which in turn belonged to the chantry of Joan Viscountess de Lisle, who lies buried under the large indent still in front of the pulpitum under the central tower. Behind the reredos in its present position, and entered from the passage above, is the secret chamber where the relics were kept. These were displayed annually on St Calixtus's Day, 14 October (see p. 9), possibly in St Calixtus's chapel, which is the chapel in this transept nearest to the pulpitum. An annual payment of 8d was made 'for bringing down the relics'; but from 1392–3 onwards the annual payment was 6d only. Does this mean that between 1347 (the date of the previous account roll) and 1392 some of the relics had had to be sold in order to meet extraordinary expenditure, for example on the scissor-arches and 'grids' in the tower? (See p. 114 below.) Against the payment of 6d in 1537–8 someone has written 'not in future'. The relics do not seem to have been very numerous. In mediaeval times the procession on Palm Sunday entering by the great west door of the cathedral had to pass under the reliquary or casket containing relics, which was held high by two of the vicars choral just inside the entrance.

At this corner are the figures of Mary and the Child, and Joseph, carved out of sycamore wood by Estcourt J Clack, originally as crib figures. In front of them is the multiple pricket or candlestand used as an aid to prayer.

In the middle of the south transept is the Saxon font brought here from the earlier cathedral, which was south of the present site, running across the present Camery and Palm Churchyard (p. 8 above). It may be in this very unusual position as a reminder that it came from the earlier cathedral. It may be that the stream crossing beneath the Palm Churchyard was used at the point now known as 'the dipping-place' as the baptistery of the old cathedral, and this would be in a similar position in the new cathedral. The inner order of the obviously semi-circular arches surrounding the font has been rather amateurishly cut in an effort to produce pointed 'Gothic' arches to match the rest of the cathedral. Dr Rodwell has also drawn attention to the remains of haloes over the heads of saints formerly carved inside each arch. The font cover was almost identical with one in St John's Church, Leeds, consecrated in 1634. But the Wells one was coloured and gilded in 1982.

*Mary and the Child Jesus, with Joseph, were carved out of sycamore by Estcourt Clack, originally as crib figures. They were considered too good to be seen only at Christmas, so they are now displayed permanently in the south transept.*

*The Saxon font, brought from the former cathedral (south of the present building). The oak cover is of c.1635.*

It is interesting to compare the bay design of the transepts with that of the nave and, in due course, with that of the quire. The double openings into the triforium are similar to the original design of the quire, where the openings were filled in in the fourteenth century, and covered with the present tabernacle work, to conform, as inexpensively as possible, with the niches in the presbytery. The width of these transept bays is much narrower than the bays in the quire—in fact, narrower by 2 ft 5 in (74 cm). This is a more satisfactory proportion, but would appear too narrow for ten, eleven or twelve in bays in the nave. So the master mason split the difference: each nave bay is 1 ft 2½ in (37 cm) wider than the transept bay, and 1 ft 2½ in (37 cm) narrower than the quire bay. Notice that the nave triforium, already described (p. 86), is derived from the design of the north and south walls of the transepts.

The chapels of St Martin and of St Calixtus in the eastern aisle were re-furnished as part of the County War Memorial of the First World War. The glass, incorporating a few old fragments, in these two chapels is by A K Nicholson, c.1922. In St Martin's chapel the Rolls of Honour of those who died in both World Wars are kept. Here also is the tomb of William Bykonyll, a prebendary of the cathedral, 1432–48. The reredos, designed by Sir Charles Nicholson, was carved by G Tosi, as part of the memorial of the First World War, and painted under the direction of Stephen Dykes Bower, Nicholson's successor as cathedral architect, as part of the memorial for the Second World War.

Tosi also carved the Crucifixion group over the altar in St Calixtus's chapel, originally as a model of the Rood (p. 88). This chapel has a tomb of c.1450 of an unidentified cleric. It is neither of Dean Husee nor of Thomas Boleyn, both of whom have had the tomb ascribed to them at one time or another. The tomb is famous for the carved alabaster panels in front: at the east end is a representation of the Annunciation. This was a theme frequently repeated by the alabaster carvers, but this is the loveliest example that has survived. Then come three canons lamenting the death of whoever lies buried here. They have been described as the best illustrations of the vestments worn by cathedral clergy at the time. The right-hand panel represents the Holy Trinity. This is the usual way the alabasterers used to depict the Trinity. The dove, to represent the Holy Spirit, was added afterwards by the silversmith. But the dove was gradually omitted, because the alabasterers found they

*ABOVE LEFT: The fifteenth-century tomb in St Calixtus's chapel has some distinguished alabaster panels on the front. On the left is one of the best of many representations of the Annunciation. The Angel Gabriel flies down to tell the praying Mary that she will bear the Child, Jesus.*

*ABOVE CENTRE: One of the weepers on the same tomb is often taken as a good example of the vestments worn by a cathedral canon at that time.*

*ABOVE RIGHT: A specimen of the conventional alabaster carving of the Trinity, from which the Holy Spirit in the form of a dove, usually supplied in silver, is missing.*

could sell their tables just as well without. Here there is no hole above the head of God the Father for the insertion of a silver dove. But there are three holes in the top right-hand corner. It has been suggested that an alabaster dove was originally fixed here, so as to balance exactly the angel Gabriel in the corresponding position at the opposite end of the tomb. This is one of the chapels reserved for private prayer.

The Saints Paul and Bartholomew in the east clerestory windows were designed by W R Eginton to go with the foreign glass in 1813 in the centre light of the great west window (p. 91). When that glass was removed in 1926, these figures were placed here. All the other windows on the south and west sides of this transept are by Powell & Co. of Whitefriars, that is to say, the windows of 1894 and 1904 in the west wall, and the lower ones of 1903 on the south side. Here the tracery lights incorporate some old glass: left to right, the arms of Thomas Holland, Earl of Kent (1350–97), half-brother of Richard II; St John the Baptist, holding an *Agnus Dei*; St John the Evangelist with a devil emerging from the poisoned cup; St Dunstan tweaking the devil's nose with a pair of tongs; and an unidentified bishop. The large south window, completed in 1905, depicting the River of the Water of Life (*Rev.* 22[1]) is a superb composition, unfortunately not easily seen because of the 'inverted arches'.

## The Scissor-Arches

This leads us to discuss at last the scissor-arches, which with their six great arches intersecting and crossing one another are best seen from outside St Calixtus's chapel. These are not, strictly speaking, strainer-arches, because their purpose is not to hold the tower piers apart or to stop them buckling under the weight of the tower. They have been criticized as useless because they are not positioned opposite the main arcades of quire, transepts and nave, and therefore do not withstand the thrust of those arcades. But they were not intended to. A good look up those piers shows that there is no bending or buckling at all: they are perfectly straight and vertical all the way. What has happened is that the two western tower-piers have sunk straight into the ground, which here is marl, whereas the two eastern piers have remained stationary, presumably standing on rock. (In fact, the north-east pier has sunk one inch (2.5 cm), which is hardly perceptible.) The result is that the lantern of the tower has split and the west side of the tower leans at the top seven inches (18 cm) out of true—not nine feet (2.7 m), as one writer has said!

The nave arcade is built on a plinth, similar to that which is visible at Salisbury, but here hidden under the paving, and noted only by those laying the pipes for the old gas lighting. There is no record of whether a similar plinth joins the piers of the crossing.

We are told that when the foundations of a building are going to fail, they do so almost at once: they do not wait for over a century before they give way. So it seems that the tower, at first built up to only 17 inches (43 cm) above roof-level (p. 61), soon started to sink on the west side, the south-west pier sinking 4 inches (10 cm), and the north-west pier only 3 inches (8 cm). As the tower sank on the west, so it pushed over the main nave arcade with it, as far as 'the break'

(see pp. 94–5), far more drastically on the south side than on the north, where it is almost imperceptible. To counteract the movement on the south, and to prevent total collapse on the raising of the walls to the full height of the nave, many pillars were built at triforium level over the main arcade on the south side only. These, which are out of sight from ground level, were all very firmly built and absolutely vertical, so as to counteract any further lateral movement. This seems to be the explanation of the multiplicity of rere-arches behind the south triforium arcade, compared with the usual arrangement of one rere-arch for every three of the triforium openings visible from the nave, which is the custom throughout the north side and in the western part (after 'the break') of the south.

When in 1313 the tower was raised to its present height, probably twice the height originally intended, and a tall spire added, the master mason, probably Thomas of Witney, inserted extra orders giving an additional 18 inches (45 cm) support to the first arch on the west side of each transept, i.e. over the nave aisles; and the first arch on each side of the nave, i.e. corresponding to the west aisles of the transepts. The new mouldings and capitals resemble Perpendicular work, but the mouldings of the bases of these inserted shafts are seen to resemble those of the Lady Chapel and retroquire, which places them in their correct time-sequence.

By 1338, it seems, although the quire extension was still unfinished and money almost exhausted, the tower was seen to have cracked so badly that a more drastic remedy was necessary. William Joy, who had succeeded Thomas as master mason in 1329 (as he was to succeed him also at Exeter in the 1340s) was the man for the job. First of all, he designed a massive flying buttress resting on the good foundations in the east, crossing the transept opening and taking a large part of the weight from the top of the western tower pier. This weight was thereby transferred from the west to the ground in the east. From new and extended foundations at the base of the western pier he built a similar arch to meet and support the first flier at the middle, to prevent it from falling on visitors' or clergy's heads, and finished off at a corresponding place on the east.

The same was done on the north side. Finally, because the south-west pier had sunk more than the north-west pier, and

*OPPOSITE: The massive scissor-arches, built c.1338–48 to support the tower when the foundations of the two western piers sank into the ground.*

also to help to relieve the weight on both western piers, similar scissor-arches were put across the nave.

William Joy's next move was to construct flying buttresses within the thickness of the wall and clearly visible crossing the lower part of the first clerestory windows of nave and transepts, to take the lateral thrust from the west corners of the tower and transfer it to the second piers of the nave, and the second piers of the transepts. In order to build these it was necessary to remove much of the original masonry. Therefore the whole tower and its tall spire must have been supported on massive baulks of timber for about ten years to allow the lime-mortar to set firmly. The workmanship of the masonry both of the scissor-arches and the in-built fliers is superb.

After the Black Death the final stage, designed by Joy but not yet executed, was to insert square 'grids' of masonry inside the tower, to hold it rigid without any twisting or other movement (see p. 64 above). All cracks were then filled with black mortar to facilitate frequent and quick inspection.

(Inverted arches were also used in the eastern transepts of Salisbury, c.1383, to transfer the thrust of the tall tower and spire downwards to the foundations further east. Scissor-arches of the Wells pattern were also inserted under the central tower of Glastonbury Abbey by Abbot Bere (1493–1524).)

The fan-vault, visible from below, was added in about 1480 by the master mason, William Smyth. The suggested reason for the construction has been offered already on page 102.

### The North Transept

The clerestory window on the east side, over the entrance to the north quire aisle, is often unnoticed. This is said to be the earliest dated example of the Renaissance style north of the Alps. The main subject is the beheading of John the Baptist; at the same time, the scenes above show Herodias sticking a bodkin or needle into the tongue of the Baptist's head, and, on the right, musicians playing in the background while a sorrowful man leans over the balustrade looking at the events below. He has been taken to be the donor of the window.

The left-hand light to make up the original three-light window was apparently already missing when the glass was bought in France in 1802 during the short-lived peace of Amiens. It probably showed Salome dancing in the upper scene, and possibly the Governor of the prison below, to balance the executioner.

*ABOVE LEFT: The string-course below the clerestory on the west side of the south transept suddenly sinks, as it was dragged down by the foundations of the south-west pillar giving way under the weight of the tower.*

*ABOVE RIGHT: Window, dated 1507, by Arnold of Nijmegen, now in the north transept clerestory, showing the beheading of St John the Baptist. In the upper scenes Herod and his wife Herodias sit with the head of the Baptist on a dish in front of them. On the right a band plays, while a sorrowful man, perhaps the donor of the window, sadly watches the events below.*

Along the top of the balustrade is the inscription:

COREGER SCET VNG GRANDT DANGĒ DETER A. LVI. SUSMIS LAN DE GRACE 1507

It has been conjectured that the complete inscription would read in modern French [*Si l'on veut un prince*] *corriger, c'est un grand danger d'être à lui sousmis.* (It is fatal to reprove a prince when you are already in his power.)

The superb features of Herodias and the sorrowful man, and the jerky movement of the executioner are typical of the work of Arnold of Nijmegen (*c*.1470–*c*.1540), who was making windows in Rouen 1502–12. The window was bought by the Dean and Chapter from a merchant in 1811–12 to help fill the centre light of the great west window in 1813. It was moved to this present unfortunate position in 1927.

In the north wall is the great window made by Powells in 1903 in memory of those who fell in the Boer War. It depicts warriors through the ages. In the right-hand light it is possible to recognize King Henry V, the Duke of Wellington, General Gordon, and perhaps one or two others from their well-known portraits. The smaller windows were designed by the same firm, but made deliberately different so as not to detract from the main windows above. They depict the kings closely associated with the early church in Somerset: Ine, Egbert, Alfred, Edward the Elder, Athelstan and Edgar.

Below the windows is the canopied memorial designed by E B Ferrey for those of the Somerset Light Infantry who fell in the South African War of 1878–9. The figure of David with the fallen Goliath behind him is the work of David Tinworth.

## The Clock

On the west wall is the clock, usually described as 'the second oldest working clock in the world'. At one time when the Salisbury clock (c.1386) was out of commission, the Wells clock was described as 'the oldest'. Both clocks were made by the same man or men. The Wells clock has some slight improvements over the Salisbury clock, including provision for the striking of the quarter-hours. It is assumed to have been made c.1390. It was certainly here from 1392 onwards (the previous surviving account-roll is for 1343–4). However, when that clock stopped in 1838, the Dean and Chapter had a new movement made, now in the church at Burnham-on-Sea. The old works, stored in the undercroft, were later moved to the Science Museum in London on long loan. There they are now, still working, and on view. At Wells the present movement dates from 1880, but visible parts, dial, quarter-jack and knights are thought to be original, though repainted since. Jack Blandiver, the quarter-jack sitting in the corner, is thought to have been made of oak c.1390, but re-painted in the seventeeth century, so as to appear to be wearing costume of the period. At every quarter-hour he kicks with his heels: ding-dong; and on the hour he hits the bell in front of him with the hammer in his right hand. At the same time as Jack kicks his heels, the horsemen start to rotate and perform the tournament

OPPOSITE: *Jack Blandiver, the quarter-jack, who strikes the bells for the quarter-hours with his heels, and hits the bell in front of him with one of his hammers on the hour.*

*The dial of the fourteenth-century clock, showing hours, position of the sun, minutes, date of the lunar month, and the phase of the moon. The four knights above rotate every time the quarter-hours are struck except during services.*

outside the castle above the dials. One knight, the same one, is killed at each rotation.

There are three dials, last re-painted in 1727, but re-varnished since. The outer dial shows two sets of twelve hours, starting with noon at the top; 1 p.m. to midnight on the right, midnight being marked by the floriated cross at the bottom; then 1 a.m. to 12 noon rising on the left. A representation of the sun takes the place of an hour-hand, which, as always in this old English system of 'a.m.' and 'p.m.', also points to the present position of the sun out-of-doors. The second circle has a star as a minute-hand. The third dial itself rotates and also has a pointer shaped like a trident or buckle, indicating the date of the *lunar* month (number of days since the new moon). Attached to the pointer is a small circle in which the actual size and angle of the moon at the present moment is shown, and this is moving very slowly all the time. All this was to ensure that choristers, vicars choral and clergy attended their services punctually. In the later Middle Ages there were so many masses going on as well as the main offices of the day, quite apart from the recital of the whole Psalter daily, that they had to be carefully dovetailed in according to a precise time-table, because no two Consecrations at Mass were allowed to take place simultaneously.

At the same time as Jack Blandiver strikes the hour, a wire which can be seen disappearing above him through the vault, rings the bell at the top of the central tower. Only this outside hour-bell was for the benefit of ordinary townspeople.

In about 1475 an outdoor clock-face was made on the corner of the transept. This also had a $2 \times 12$-hour dial until about 1830 when the present outside clock-face was made. There are also two knights, whose armour gives the approximate date of their carving: *c*.1475. They strike the quarters. A new window in the vicars' kitchen on the other side of the road shows the purpose of that dial: to let the vicars in their Hall know when it was time for them to go across the recently-built Chain Bridge and down the Chapter House stairs to service (p. 66).

Underneath the clock inside is the figure of Christ, carved in yew-wood by Estcourt Clack in 1954, in a form reminiscent of the Crucifixion, the Resurrection (grave-clothes hanging loose) and the Ascension.

The capital on the left (south) of the clock inside has a head with tooth-ache; two combined bird-dragons; head of a baboon; and a man wearing a cap. Among the foliage is a raspberry or strawberry still with original red paint on it. The capital on the right of the clock shows Moses holding the tablets of the Law, Aaron, and a man writing a scroll with the letters AIA. The capital in the corner under Jack Blandiver has a man carrying a goose; another tooth-ache face; and two other heads in the vestry. The responds at triforium level well repay inspection.

The pulpitum or quire-screen was made in about 1335. It is possible to see, especially on the south side, that the scissor-arch was inserted after the screen-wall was already in position. The niches were then filled with statues of Kings of England, as at Canterbury, York and so on. Here they would have held the statues of all the kings from William I to Edward III, excluding the usurper, Stephen. Much later two vicars choral who misbehaved were ordered as punishment 'to re-paint a king'. The middle section of the screen was most regrettably pushed out to accommodate the greatly enlarged organ, completed in 1857. This was done by Anthony Salvin, the architect, although he had strongly opposed it.

### The South Quire Aisle

The quire is entered by the main doors under the screen only at times of service. At other times entry is made by one of the aisle doors. These may be inspected en route, as all the doors in the cathedral, except three, are original. The aisle doors were made at the same time as the stone screens of the transept aisles in the last quarter of the fourteenth century.

For the purpose of this description it will be convenient to enter by the south aisle. On the right side is an alabaster effigy of John Harewell, Bishop 1366–86, who gave two bells called after him, a previous great west window, and two-thirds of the cost of the south-west tower. At his feet, to represent his name, are two hares and the formal representation of a spring or well.

On the left are three effigies of Saxon bishops, part of a set of seven. The bishops were formerly buried around the quire of the old cathedral in the Camery (see pp. 7–8, and 77–8). Soon after the quire of the present cathedral was opened for service, shortly after 1200, the bishop asked for the bones of all his predecessors to be placed in the equivalent positions round his new quire. It then extended over the crossing and into the first bay of the present nave. (You can see that the bases on the east side of the first pillars and wall-shafts of the nave aisles have been made good where the upright posts of the wooden screens and doors fitted in.) The bones were re-boxed and a lead label inserted with each, so as to ensure that the right bones were in the right box. New stone boxes were made in which the wooden boxes were placed and new effigies carved on the lids to represent 'old bishops'. When the quire was moved eastwards in the fourteenth century, so these tombs and their contents were transferred round the new quire. But the Victorians did not like them, and removed them to the undercroft because they looked 'untidy'. At the same time the railings and reredos of Bekynton's chantry were removed also on the grounds of being 'out of line' and irregular. Bekynton's reredos was moved into the then unused chapel of St Calixtus, and a stove-pipe driven through one end of it. The bishops' tombs were moved back into their present positions by Dean Armitage Robinson in 1913, when new wooden boxes were made for the bones and new stone boxes to hold the wooden ones. In 1978 the contents of the boxes were examined by Dr Warwick Rodwell, with the permission of the Dean and Chapter, and found to be in a very confused state. The bones were sorted by the pathologist, Dr Juliet Rogers, so that each bishop now has the correct number of limbs, and everything was carefully replaced. Because the effigies, made long after the subjects died, have flat bases and canopies to keep the rain and the pigeons off, Dr Rodwell has assumed that they were designed as standing figures, possibly on some screen. The one tomb which is unnamed has no lead label; but since all the others are named, we still know that the right bones are in the right box.

The raised slab, with a perspex cover, is that covering the coffin of William Bytton II, Bishop 1267–74. This is said to be one of the earliest incised slabs in the country. The stone is blue lias, which is used for most of the memorial slabs and indents of brasses at Wells. One of the very few slabs of Purbeck marble in the cathedral is that of George Hooper, Bishop 1704–27, which is adjacent. His wife, next to him, is buried beneath a slab of blue lias. Next beyond Bytton is the sumptuous tomb of Lord Arthur Hervey, Bishop 1869–94, the sarcophagus in pink alabaster by J L Pearson, and the effigy in carrara marble by Sir Thomas Brock. So many young visitors stroke the lion cub at the bishop's feet with their sticky fingers, that it has to be washed quite frequently. Then, on the floor, behind the bishop's throne, is the brass of Arthur Lake, Bishop 1616–26 (see p. 27 above).

# THE QUIRE

When one enters by the main doors under the organ the effect is rather that of bursting from the fairly plain nave into a blaze of colour, produced by the stained glass in the eastern windows and the glorious needlework of the stalls.

## Needlework

The needlework of the quire was almost wholly designed by Alice, Lady Hylton, and executed by ladies and some men of the diocese between 1937 and 1949, very largely during the war-time 'black-out'. The scheme of decoration of the hangings of the prebendal stalls, running anti-clockwise from the dean's stall (inside the entrance on the south) to that of the precentor (inside the entrance to the north), is the sequence of bishops' arms in chronological order, alternately red and blue, interrupted by special descriptive designs on gold backgrounds for the stalls of the dignitaries—dean, chancellor, archdeacon of Wells, treasurer, precentor; and of the two other archdeacons. Below them are designs collected from a variety of sources by Lady Hylton, who also herself obtained the wool coloured with natural dyes, which are less subject to fading, and dictated the stitches to be used. Visitors come from overseas to inspect them, and it is they who have pointed out to us that these are the first to use a variety of stitches, sometimes as many as six different ones on the same canvas, whereas previously elsewhere, they say, one stitch was chosen and used throughout.

## The Design

We have the same chance to admire both the needlework and the stained glass if we enter the quire from one of the side aisles. The east wall of the church, where work began c.1180, was on a line between the present bishop's throne and the pulpit. East of this (where we enter) was an ambulatory, and possibly a one-bay Lady Chapel beyond, both no higher than the aisles. The arrangement was probably very similar to that of Abbey Dore in Herefordshire.

The design of the compound pillars and arch-mouldings in the original quire persists right down to the west end of the church. At first the capitals are low; with each pair, as we move from east to west, the height is increased, until in the transepts the height of $20\frac{1}{2}$ inches (52 cm) is arrived at, and retained throughout the nave.

The triforium design consisted of two openings, slightly wider than, but otherwise resembling, those in the transepts. Their outlines, with later infilling, can be seen from the triforium passage under the aisle roof.

Work on extending the old quire eastward by three bays *plus* the retroquire, to meet the completed new Lady Chapel, must have begun at foundation level not later than 1320 (see pp. 19 and 79). The purpose was to locate the whole of the liturgical quire in the eastern arm, east of the crossing. Work was slow, the eastern transept, at aisle height, not being reached until *c*.1329.

The old east wall (between present throne and pulpit) seems to have been removed in 1333, when the Dean and Chapter forecast at least a further three years' work. In fact, it is evident that the quire was not completed until *c*.1340. In 1338 when all the best masons were put on to the work of supporting the central tower, some inferior work was done at clerestory level. Where the clerestory windows in Decorated style replaced the original lancets, the new ashlar was not aligned properly with the old either inside or out. Yet some of these stones bear a mason's mark not observed in the building before or since. He was obviously, therefore, not an apprentice, since an apprentice was not allowed a mark until he had completed his articles. Was he therefore a very old mason, partially blind, recalled from retirement to fill the vacancy? The design of the three westerly clerestory windows is very weak. This is not wholly the fault of the master mason. For cusps have been carelessly hacked off, perhaps with an axe, to simplify the re-glazing. This may have been during the period of the Commonwealth, when contrary to expectation, some of the windows were re-glazed under the 'Preacher', Cornelius Burges.

## The Stained Glass

People often ask why it is that the western windows of the quire, which were undoubtedly also filled with stained glass, were destroyed—either by the Parliamentary troops or by the Monmouth rebels—while the more easterly ones were not. The answer seems to be that in the presbytery, where the walls are thinner, the passage is very narrow and the parapet only a few inches high. So a drunken soldier swinging his pike to destroy the windows was just as likely himself to fall inwards as the glass to fall outwards. When this happened at the first clerestory windows of the presbytery on each side, the men following turned back. Now there is a hand-rail of piping along the passage openings, but this was only placed there in 1913 to help Dean Robinson (and others) when inspecting the windows.

The glass which was saved in the east end is one of the great glories of Wells, and among the most splendid fourteenth-century glass anywhere. In the early morning when the sun is shining, the splendour of the east window is almost unbelievable; on a dull day and even quite late in the evening the colours are still superb. It is often known as the Golden Window, because of the extensive use of silver stain, in addition to much yellow, red and green glass, and only a very small quantity of blue. It can be dated to c.1340. It is a Jesse window, and shows Jesse at the bottom of the centre light, wearing a red and yellow skirt, and a green shirt, resting his head on his hand against the mullion on his right (our left). From him issue the tendrils of a vine (with reference to *Isaiah* $11^1$), which loop around the descendants of Jesse and his ancestors back to Abraham. So we see the Madonna and Child in the centre of the window, immediately above Jesse; David with his harp on their right (our left); and Solomon holding a model of the Temple in Jerusalem, which he built, on our right. It may be observed that the Temple is shown with a spire, since all English cathedral towers were intended to have spires until the Wells south-west tower was built some fifty years later (see p. 52). Immediately over these central figures is the Crucifixion (unusual in a Jesse window), with the mother of Jesus on one side and St John on the other. All the figures have their names underneath in Lombardic script in the spelling of the Vulgate. All those named, except the prophets Daniel and Ezekiel, occur in the genealogy of Christ in *Matthew*, chapter 1. (Perhaps Ezechiel, which is made up of fragments, should be Ezechias, *Matt*.1[9,10].)

The persons represented in the side clerestory windows are as follows, from left to right:

*Window over the pulpit*, designed by Joseph Bell of Bristol, 1851, (possibly the only bad window in the cathedral): St Augustine, St Ambrose, St Athanasius.

*Window 2*: St Richard of Chichester, St Giles, St Gregory. This and the next window were inserted c.1345.

*Window 3*, nearest the east window: St Blaise, St George and St Leo.

On the south side: *Window 1*, nearest the east window: St

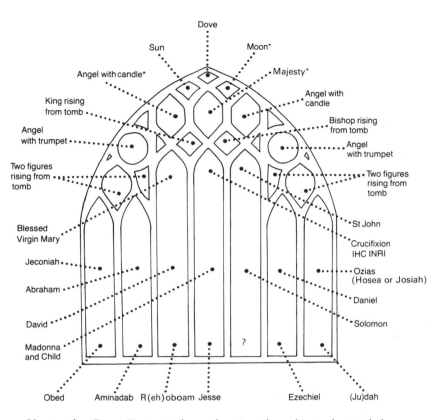

*Key to the Great East window, showing the subjects depicted there.*
*\* denotes a modern replacement.*

Clement, St Edward the Confessor (?), St Ethelbert. This
and the next window were inserted *c.*1345.
*Window 2*: St Brice, St Ambrose, St Wulstan.
*Window 3*: made by T H Willement in 1846. A comparison of
this window with the east window of the Lady Chapel,

which he only restored in 1845, shows how much old glass, especially in the canopies, was retained in the latter. Here the canopies are over-simplified and crude. The figures are St Patrick, St Dunstan and St Benignus, all associated with Glastonbury.

### The Victorian Restoration

Below the window (more or less) is the Bishop's Throne or *cathedra* (which makes this a *cathedral* church), *c*.1340. Salvin in his restoration of the quire *c*.1850 made two minor changes to the design of the throne. These are distinguishable (a) by comparison with old prints, and (b) by Salvin's use of Bath stone instead of Doulting, which he had apparently never heard of; just as he also used Purbeck marble to replace blue lias. The front of the throne, where the bishop's desk is, formerly bulged forward in a curve. Salvin set it back in a straight line. At the top of the canopy over the throne, there are towers, one on each side, with flat tops, rather like the cathedral's western towers. The present tops were the bases of spirelets, resembling the one in the centre between the two 'towers'. For some reason Salvin raised the bases on white 'legs' of Bath stone, and did away with the spirelets. Otherwise, the throne remains very much as first built. It is unlikely that the niches ever contained statues.

The niches which surround the presbytery at triforium level certainly never had statues. There is no sign of anything having stood there and no sign of fixing. Also it is known that money was extremely short at this time of building. The master mason, William Joy, obviously wanted to create big shadows in order to increase the sense of lightness.

Of the statues under the east window, the three in the middle, Christ with St Peter and St Andrew, were carved by A G Walker and given by Mrs Jessie Head in memory of her brother, Douglas McLean, before the First World War; the remainder were given after the First World War, those on the north (St Patrick and St Dunstan), carved by E C Burton, were also given by Mrs Head; those on the south, St David and St George, also carved by E C Burton, were given by Somerset Freemasons in memory of their members who died in that war.

Anthony Salvin's restoration of the quire began in 1848. The wooden canopies over the prebendal stalls, probably like the stalls of Chichester or Hereford with a straight top of

*ABOVE LEFT: An 1823 engraving, of part of the quire, showing the bishop's throne and prebendal stalls (with gallery over) before the Victorian restoration.*

*ABOVE RIGHT: The bishop's throne, Victorian stalls and twentieth-century wool embroidery, as they are now.*

battlements or brattishing, had already been spoilt in the sixteenth century by the addition of timber galleries on top with Perpendicular traceried fronts, much of which has since been re-used for reredoses and barriers (see below pp. 135–7). The galleries had to be removed because the timber supports and stairs of softwood leading to them occupied much of the space of the quire aisles, and were extremely unsightly as well as inconvenient. When the galleries were removed, the problem was how to provide seating for those who had been accommodated there. The architect's solution was to set back the wall behind the back stalls, and put in a new row for the prebendaries between the pillars. The old back row, which ran immediately in front of the pillars had to be moved forward slightly, and gangways made. Some of the misericords of the old back row were thereby displaced, and could not be fitted in the blank spaces, because there is a considerable difference in their sizes. Three of those displaced are exhibited in the

.retroquire (see below pp. 132–3). One was given to the Victoria & Albert Museum in London. Misericord no. 63 was placed under the Dean's stall by order of Dean Edwards in 1972.

## The Misericords

Seats should not be lifted without permission, as if this is done without first removing the cushions, the hinges and screws will be forced. And the cushions must be replaced correctly. Moreover, the misericords are almost impossible to see without kneeling down and using a torch. They are most easily studied from the picture-book published by the Friends of Wells Cathedral (the numbers refer to this). The subjects of all the misericords, made c.1335, are as follows:

1. Goat (broken).
2. Griffin and lion fighting.
3. Man in hood and drawers riding bareback facing horse's tail.
4. Hawk preying on rabbit.
5. Mermaid (unfinished).
6. Two crossbills in a pine-tree.
7. Ape mimicking a pedlar (broken).
8. Double-bodied monster.
9. Griffin with dog's head.
10. Two goats butting.
11. Monkey holding an owl (unfinished).
12. Two wyverns interlocked, each biting the other's tail.
13. Ewe suckling a lamb (unfinished).
14. Wyvern and horse fighting.
15. Mermaid suckling a lion.
16. Man with cup asking his wife for more.
17. Cat and mouse (unfinished).
18. Bat-winged monster.
19. Griffin eating a lamb.
20. Puppy biting a cat (unfinished).
21. Tumbler.
22. Dog.
23. Cat playing the fiddle (broken).
24. Man stabbing head of dragon.
25. Bust of bishop wearing amice, chasuble and mitre (unfinished).
26. Peacock.
27. Fox preaching to four geese, one asleep.
28. Cock crowing.
29. Sleeping lion.
30. Dragon, apparently asleep, with wings expanded.
31. Man squatting, with hands on knees.
32. Fox and goose.
33. Head of a man with ass's ears.
34. Two monsters with male and female heads caressing (unfinished).

35. Man supporting the seat with hand and foot.
36. Lion with ass's ears.
37. Bird scratching its head.
38. Sleeping cat (unfinished).
39. Man waking and stretching.
40. Dragon (or wyvern) with hairy belly, biting its back.
41. Two ducks conversing.
42. Two dragons fighting (unfinished).
43. Bat's head (unfinished).
44. Hairy man with lion's legs.
45. Old woman with hands clasped, lying on her side.
46. Tumbler about to turn somersault.
47. Head of a lady with ornate hairstyle and veil.
48. Lion.
49. Bat.
50. Head and shoulder of female angel.
51. Lion.
52. Two birds about to drink from ewer which stands in a basin (unfinished).
53. Monkey holds squirrel with collar and lead.
54. Wood-pigeon.

55. Man riding and whipping a lion.
56. Cat passing a pig (broken).
57. Eagle (unfinished).
58. Head and shoulders of a man who supports the seat with his hands.
59. Rabbit.
60. Two-legged beast looking at its tail, which sprouts foliage.
61. Man, left-handed, killing a dragon (wyvern). (Mounted on retroquire wall. See below, p. 133.)
62. Boy pulling a thorn from his foot. (Replacement of 1664, mounted on retroquire wall. See p. 133.)
63. Pelican in its piety. (In the dean's stall.)
64. Alexander the Great being carried up to heaven by two griffins tempted by a piece of meat. (Mounted on retroquire wall. See p. 133.)
65. Crouching figure, with feet curled beneath him, elbows raised to level of head. (V & A Museum, London, no. W. 48–1912.)

For those who are not familiar with misericords a word of explanation may be useful. The canons and their vicars were expected to take part in services lasting from shortly after midnight almost without a break until midday or beyond. There were eight main offices of the day, as well as several

*View of the quire, showing the organ-case of 1974.*

masses, and the whole Psalter of 150 psalms was recited daily, in addition to the psalms for the day as set as part of the daily offices. For the psalms, singing and prayers they had to stand. This was very tiring for such long periods without a break, and they felt sorry for one another. Hence the word 'misericord', which means 'pity' or 'feeling sorry'. The seats were hinged at the back and could be lifted, revealing a ledge built out from the underside, on which canons and vicars could rest their buttocks. They could therefore sit while appearing to stand. There is a legend that if anyone fell asleep during the service, the seat would fall with a crash, which not only woke the offender, but also drew attention to him. However, this is not true of the Wells stalls. As originally hinged, the seats would not fall of their own accord.

The altar rails, designed by Stephen Dykes Bower, were given by public subscription in memory of Richard Malden, Dean 1933–50, and replaced some very ornate Victorian brass ones, which in turn took the place of fairly simple Jacobean wooden rails. The kneelers in front of the altar rails were designed by Mrs Pat Russell to match the Minton tiles of the sanctuary, and made by the cathedral embroiderers in 1982.

Very soon after the pulpitum was built, about 1335, an organ was placed on it. But we possess no details of the successive organs there, although frequent mentions of them occur from about 1400 onwards. It is not until after the Restoration that we have a contract dated 3 July 1662 for the making of a new organ by Robert Taunton at a cost of £800 or less, with eight stops on the Great and six stops on the Chaire organ. A coloured drawing of this organ, completed in 1664, with a case very similar to the present one at Gloucester, survives in the library of the Royal College of Organists. Subsequent repairs and additions of new stops were made by Renatus Harris and Thomas Swarbrick. In 1786 the organ was completely repaired and enlarged by Samuel Green at a cost of £420. As a result of this rebuild the organ now had 10 stops on the Great, 5 on the Chair or Choir organ, and 6 on the Swell. That organ was replaced by an almost completely new instrument made by Henry Willis, completed in 1857, for which the centre part of the pulpitum was extended on the west side. This organ had no case and was extremely ugly. It was rebuilt and enlarged in 1910 by Harrison & Harrison of Durham, who again rebuilt it in 1973–4, with 4,630 pipes and 67 speaking stops. On this occasion the Friends of Wells Cathedral, by

means of a special 'whip-round' among its members, paid for a
case for the organ, designed by Alan Rome, the present
cathedral architect. The Friends' normal income from subscriptions and legacies is mainly devoted to essential repairs to
the fabric, so the Friends' policy required a special collection in
this instance, as for the statue of Christ on the West Front (p.
50).

## South Quire Aisle (Continued)

It may now be convenient to return to the south quire aisle by
the door beyond the bishop's throne. When going out of the
quire, notice the doors, and especially the hinges of c.1340.
These are a typical local design, which persisted in Somerset
until the sixteenth century. We come at once to the chantry
chapel of Thomas Bekynton, Bishop 1443–65, whose building
activities have already been described (p. 22). His effigy is of
alabaster, on which the paint has been renewed periodically, on
a table-tomb over the cadaver, both of Bath stone (painted).
This type of monument, known as a *memento mori* ('Remember
you must die') was common for about fifty years in the
fifteenth century; and must have served as a reminder to
Bekynton to be on his best behaviour. He placed his tomb here
fifteen years before he died. An American visitor, pointing to
the cadaver, said: 'That's his poor wife, I presume.' He had to
be disillusioned. Bekynton gave the city its water supply, in
return for which the City Council visited his chantry annually
on 20 September—the date of the gift—and said prayers for his
soul. Now the councillors attend Evensong on 14 January, the
anniversary of his death.

The reredos of this chantry was removed by the Victorians,
as already mentioned (p. 121) into the empty chapel of St
Calixtus. It was restored to its proper position here in 1922.
The colouring was restored by Maurice Keevil in 1948. At the
extreme north-east corner, and visible only from the altar step
is the appealing little figure of Bekynton's jester, looking very
woebegone at his master's death. The ironwork of the chantry,
local work of 1450, is very commendable workmanship, and
similar to the railings round the tomb of Sir Thomas Hungerford in the chapel of Farleigh Hungerford Castle, on the
border of Somerset and Wiltshire.

Beyond Bekynton is the effigy of Dudoc, Bishop 1033–60, a
late effigy of the series of Saxon bishops.

Fixed to the wall just beyond this effigy are three misericords, displaced when they were all re-arranged in the course of the Victorian restoration. The top two were carved *c*.1335: (1) Alexander the Great is carried up to heaven by two griffins tempted (on the donkey-and-carrot principle) by a piece of meat carried on Alexander's (broken) spear. (2) St George kills the dragon with a spear in his left hand. (Dragon-killers tend to be left-handed in Somerset.) (3) In 1664 the Dean and Chapter ordered each prebendary to repair his own seat, some of the misericords having gone for firewood during the Commonwealth period. This prebendary evidently made his own carving of a boy removing a large thorn from his foot. It is not entirely satisfactory, but he tried. One other fourteenth-century misericord was given to the Victoria and Albert Museum. The other sixty-one misericords are in position under the stalls in the quire, as already described (pp. 128–131).

The windows of the south quire aisle date from the early fourteenth century, when they took the place of the original lancets. The tracery lights of the first window from the west have glass depicting the Coronation of the Virgin by Our Lord, with censing angels. The inscription in the main light, *dna Alesia: C(om)itissa can(tii)* in black-letter is a replacement of 1982, the original having been broken in that year by vandals. John Carter claimed he saw in 1794: *Orate pro anima Alesie comitisse Cantie et dom* . . . (Pray for the soul of Alice, Countess of Kent, and lady . . .). It is probable that grisaille patterned glass filled all the main lights, since the object of the enlarged windows was to admit more light to the quire. The second window from the west has a very beautiful little Crucifixion in the tracery, together with the donor of the window, who is shown saying (in Latin): 'May the passion of Our Lord Jesus Christ be our salvation and protection'.The cross is green, to symbolize the Tree of Life. Our Lord is wearing a fillet around his head to represent the Crown of Thorns in the form of the wreath of rushes, acquired by Louis IX in the Crusades. (The Sainte Chapelle in Paris was built to contain this, and it is now preserved in the Treasury of Notre Dame.)

Neither of these windows uses silver-stain, of which more will be said below (pp. 140–1). The third window contains an assembly of later heraldic glass, and seventeenth-century panels from the Netherlands based on old prints identified by Dr William Cole. The last and first three are based on the story of Abraham (*Gen.* 12–24), while numbers 4, 5, 6 (in the reverse order) illustrate Our Lord's parable of the unmerciful servant

(*Matt.* 18$^{23-5}$). At the top of the window is the earliest coloured representation of the arms of the see; at the bottom the earliest representation of the arms of the Dean and Chapter. The next window, also without silver-stain shows in the tracery-lights the Virgin and Child, with censing angels. Jesus fingers his mother's chin, and holds a small bird in his other hand. The last window before the chapel shows St Michael with a red cross shield, like that of St George, since both were dragon-killers. This one is right-handed. Another using the same cartoon reversed is in the north quire aisle opposite.

### St Katherine's Chapel

These small chapels are used in turn for the Holy Communion service on weekdays. At the entry to the chapel is the tomb of John Drokensford (Droxford), Bishop 1309–29, on which most of the colouring is original. This tomb had a high stone canopy which was removed in 1758, being considered unsafe. It has been observed that this tomb contains almost every type of stone used in the cathedral: the effigy of Bath stone, painted, rests on a slab of Purbeck marble, which is supported on the tomb-chest of Bath stone on a platform of blue lias, on a base of Doulting stone. In the same chapel is the tomb of John Gunthorpe, Dean 1472–98. The iron bar running along part of the top of this tomb seems to have held prickets for candles which burnt before an image called Jessina, which seems to have been a Nativity scene of Mary and the child Jesus, given by Gunthorpe himself.

Under the west window is a very interesting little late brass on the wall, in memory of Humphrey Willis, 1618. The picture presented is full of interest, showing Mr Willis's hobbies, the 'whole armour of God', as described in *Ephesians* 6; the Tetragrammaton (4 letters of the Hebrew name of God) and so on, all worth examining carefully. The brass purports to have been put up by Humphrey Willis's widow. But it seems to have been erected, in fact, by her cousin, Thomas Popham, who subsequently married her. The Latin inscription has been well translated by the late Mr Justice (Lord) Coleridge, as recorded alongside.

The west window above contains fifteenth-century quarries of daisies and birds painted in grisaille and silver-stain, collected at some time from various parts of the cathedral and arranged formally in the centre light by Dennis King. They would have looked better at the foot of each light, and been easier to see if spaced with a blank quarry between each pictorial one.

The south window has some of the very interesting foreign glass acquired in 1813 to fill the centre light of the great west window, removed from there in 1926 and inserted here in 1931, and recently cleaned and re-ordered. The three lights on the left belonged to a window, probably in the church of St John the Evangelist in Rouen, illustrating the legendary life of St John, as related in the *Golden Legend*. Two more lights from the same window, which went to Costessey and then to America, returned to England and were bought by the Friends of Wells Cathedral for the east window of this chapel in 1954. Three lights of the same series which were also at Costessey are now in the Burrell Collection in Glasgow, and some others in the west window of Ely Cathedral. They are thought to be the work of a pupil of Arnold of Nijmegen, sometimes described as 'The Master of St Vincent, Rouen'. The right-hand light of our south window, which depicts St John asleep in a park, seeing in his vision the seven golden candlesticks, and the Emperor Domitian as Antichrist, comes from the same church, but a different window, and is perhaps the work of Arnold of Nijmegen himself. The designs of candlesticks and Domitian closely follow woodcuts by Arnold's friend, Albrecht Dürer. They used to swap drawings.

In the east window there are two ovals of French sixteenth-century glass, acquired later by the Friends of Wells Cathedral. Unfortunately, they have been put in the wrong way: Joseph should be at the bottom. Glass is always read from the bottom (the part nearest to the viewer) upwards.

The reredos of this chapel is composed of fragments of late Perpendicular wooden tracery which formed the front of the galleries erected over the prebendal stalls, with much untidy timber occupying the quire aisles, to accommodate ladies at services in the quire after the Reformation. In the middle of this is a fine piece of carving, unfortunately obscured by the recent thick gilding. This is Flemish work of the second half of the seventeenth century, and no record exists of how it came to Wells. One recalls that our Bishop Ken (Bishop 1685–91) had at one time been Chaplain to Mary, the daughter of James II, married to William of Orange, so that she became Queen regnant when William became king of England as William III. In his capacity of chaplain at The Hague Ken had succeeded George Hooper (Bishop of Bath and Wells 1704–27). So it

may be through either of these connections that this altarpiece came to Wells. In the centre is the Crucifixion. The left-hand panel depicts the Betrayal in the Garden. Peter cuts off the ear of Malchus, who, as often, is represented as the lamp bearer. He is shown with a grinning face. This scene seems to have been frequently influenced by the mediaeval drama in which Malchus, like the porter in *Macbeth*, provided comic relief in that intensely dramatic scene. The right-hand panel represents the Harrowing of Hell (1 *Pet.* $3^{19}$) in which on Holy Saturday Jesus, carrying the oriflamme, is shown bringing out of the jaws of Hell the souls of those worthies who had died before their redemption by Christ on the cross. First of those to be brought out by Him were Adam and Eve.

### The Chapel of St John the Baptist

The adjoining chapel of St John the Baptist has a reredos made by Sir Charles Nicholson out of the same late Perpendicular tracery. The big chest is the old chest in which the Chapter Seal was kept. A seal measures not more, as a rule, than $3 \times 2$ inches ($7.5 \times 5$ cm). It can be easily slipped in a pocket, or hidden in the hand, and carried away. This chest is not so easy to move without being noticed. A seal–chest normally has a narrow ledge inside on which the seal is actually kept, the remaining space being used to keep valuable books and documents.

There is no firm evidence to show whose grave is marked by the lofty tomb between this chapel and the Lady Chapel. It is not the tomb of Bishop William Bytton I (Bishop 1248–64), which was 'of blew marble' in the centre of the Lady Chapel and taken down before 1727. But it might well be that of John Marcel or Martel, canon 1316–*c*.1343, Chancellor of the diocese under Drokensford and Bishop's Official under Shrewsbury. His obit was celebrated in St Katherine's chapel.

The east window is filled with glass of *c*.1330, which is still intact in the upper half of the window, as well as much of the bottom row of panels. But the centre is now filled with fragments. On the flyleaf of Ludolphus's *Life of Christ* in the cathedral library there is a note written by an observer, who recorded that on 8 April 1642 immediately after Richard Allen's institution in the quire to the vicarage of Batcombe, Somerset, with a friend from London,

*OPPOSITE: View across the retroquire to St John the Baptist's chapel and the Lady Chapel.*

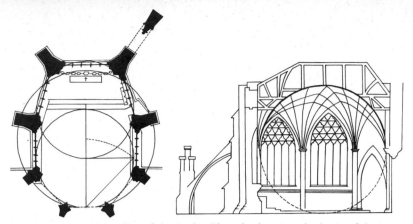

*ABOVE LEFT: Plan of the Lady Chapel, showing the basis of design.*
*ABOVE RIGHT: A section through the Lady Chapel.*

'there being a very faire crucifix at the upper end of the
south end of the Cathedrall church behinde the Quier,
this Londoner most moliciously threw a stone at it &
broke it'.

The blue sky of the centre panel marks all that remains of that
crucifixion scene.

### The Retroquire

This most attractive space may have been conceived with a
saint's shrine behind the High Altar in mind, with plenty of
room for processions and the passage of pilgrims. The thin
pillars with their tierceron ribs, combined with a lierne vault,
are reminiscent of a copse of palm trees. Additional tiercerons
spring from the main pillars on each side to fill an awkward
gap; but there is nowhere for them to go, so the master mason
has summoned two lions' heads to bite them off.

### The Lady Chapel

This is built in the form of an irregular octagon, and was at first
a separate, free-standing building, separated by grass from the
old east end. But it had been very carefully measured out from
the old east end, so that it is perfectly aligned on the old work.
Its plan can be simply fitted in between two equal overlapping
circles, within a larger circle, of which the radius equals the
square root of twice the square of the radius of the small circles.
And that large circle turned on edge produces an east-west
section showing the vault, which is a perfect semi-circle in this
plain, with the circumference at its lowest point exactly
touching the middle of the floor.

*The Lady Chapel vault, c.1320. The painted decoration was devised and executed at his own expense by Thomas Willement in 1845. It was repaired and cleaned in 1978.*

The vault is a star vault, popular in the south-west of England, with the bosses depicting the same plants concentrically (in an oval), i.e. working outwards from the centre, vine, acanthus, oak, rose. The vault was painted by Thomas Willement in 1845. He had already restored the chapel's east window and his bill had been paid (which did not always happen). To show his gratitude and his appreciation of the building, he offered to paint the vault free of charge. He submitted five designs, preserved in the cathedral library, for the Dean and Chapter to choose from; and they chose the largest. The vault was repaired and the limewash renewed in 1978, and the paint—mostlyWillement's original paint—was touched up at the expense of the Friends of Wells Cathedral, who were also responsible for the cleaning, repair and limewashing of all the low vaults in the eastern arm. At the same time the small organ, built by Sweetland of Bath c.1860, was reinstated. The experts were instructed to strip the varnish from the case and stain the pitch-pine to look like natural oak. When they stripped the varnish, they found it actually was natural oak, stained to look like pitch-pine!

The windows are of particular interest. First of all, the tracery consists of a series of spherical triangles spiked, like Pelion upon Ossa, one above the other. But in each case the base is half the thickness or width of the sides. The result is that when you look up from ground-level, you can see practically the whole of the stained glass in these openings: Old Testament patriarchs on the north-east; Christian saints on the south-east. Also, in the glass in these tracery openings there is a complete absence of silver-stain; moreover, the white glass of the eyes had to be leaded into the coloured glass of the faces, so that they appear to be wearing spectacles. Between 1310 and 1320 somebody discovered that the application of any compound of silver on to white glass produces a yellow tint when fired in the oven, which becomes darker if the quantity is increased or the period of firing extended. News of this discovery swept across Europe like wildfire, so that it is a valid tenet that a coloured window in which yellow appears on a piece of glass which is partially white must have been made after 1310 and probably after c.1320; and a window in which any yellows are produced only by the use of yellow pot-metal glass, i.e. without the use of silver-stain, will probably be before 1320.

In the Lady Chapel no silver-stain is used in the tracery lights. These are usually glazed while the scaffold is still up. So they were almost certainly glazed before 1320. On the other hand, the canopies of the main lights, most of which are still in their original condition and undamaged, are made of white glass, to which silver-stain (yellow) has been applied. Main lights are not usually filled until all the building work is completed, for fear of accidental damage; and sometimes have to wait several years until additional funds have been raised or a generous donor comes forward. In either case, we can safely say that the main lights were not filled until after 1320. We know for a fact that the Lady Chapel had been finished by 1326, but this fact by itself means little, since the chapel was still described as 'new' in c.1408.

The glass which now fills the main lights comes from all parts of the eastern arm of the cathedral, having been knocked out in the seventeenth century. The lights of all the aisle windows and the east windows of the south transept have the same width, 2 ft. 3 ins. (68 cm), so the inscription now in the south-east window of the Lady Chapel which says, 'This is the chapel of St Katherine . . .' obviously came from St Katherine's chapel in the south-east transept; and the inscription referring to Dean Edward Husee, who died in 1305, possibly comes from the east window of St Calixtus's chapel, where Husee's chantry was, in the main south transept. Dr John Harvey has suggested that the canons' names collected in the Lady Chapel glass always belonged here and record the names of contributors to the building scheme which began with the completion of the Chapter House. The arms of Roger Mortimer and the inscriptions to him and William of Littleton in the north window do not belong here. In 1686 they were seen in the east aisle of the north transept. We do not know where the arms of Zouche originated.

As already mentioned, the east window was repaired by Willement in 1845, the cost being met by Dean Goodenough personally. The tracery lights and canopies are original, also parts of some of the figures. What Willement actually did was described by him as follows:

'1845.—The fine centre window of the Lady Chapel taken down, cleaned, releaded and refixed. Several new figures of Prophets &c &c added where the old were imperfect.'

The work was well done. The chief cause for complaint is the too intense and unbroken blue and red of the backgrounds of the figures.

No record has been found of when the windows were filled with fragments. The south-east window was partially re-arranged by Dean Armitage Robinson, so as to give the appearance of figures. The large pieces of glass in pastel shades which appear in some of the lower lights of the north-east and south-east windows belong to the fragment of French glass bought by the cartload by George Henry Law, Bishop 1824–45, for the adornment of the palace.

The reredos is much mutilated. During the latter part of the last century it was thought to be the one removed from behind the High Altar in 1758 as unsafe, but it is now thought to have been made for its present position. It looks wrong because the restorers in 1844 added an extra altar step, with the result that the lower niches appear to be at floor-level. The sedilia belong to the Victorian restoration: none appear on old prints. But the door is original, though the head-stops must be new.

The large brass lectern, given by Robert Creyghtone, the Dean, in 1661, now stands at the entrance to the Lady Chapel, as shown in many old prints. When there was no heating in the cathedral (four stoves to heat the whole building were first bought in 1869), weekday services were sung in the Lady Chapel and that is probably why the lectern was moved here. The Bible, printed extremely well at the Cambridge University Press in 1660, and still in use up to 1966, is in the cathedral library. It is in two volumes, one for each side of the lectern, which should be turned sideways, so that the reader, standing at the side, can speak to the congregation on his left or right. When the lectern was in general use in the nave, the canons tried to read over the top of the lectern, which is impossible and never intended. It was made by William Borroughes of London, who subsequently made the lecterns for Canterbury and Lincoln Cathedrals and Queen's College, Oxford.

Not far from the lectern and fixed in a frame to the back of the wall behind the High Altar is the embroidered hood of a cope. Although this looks like typical seventeenth-century work, the staff of the Victoria and Albert Museum assures us that it is Victorian. It appeared suddenly in the 1930s, but no

OPPOSITE: *The lectern, given by Robert Creyghtone (I), Dean 1660–70, Bishop 1670–72, in 1661, and made by William Borroughes of London, who made the lecterns of Canterbury Cathedral and elsewhere.*

record of its provenance exists. At the north-east corner of the same wall are some examples of very fine altar lace made by Mrs C M Town from 1958 to 1966, and given by her to the cathedral in memory of her daughter who died on active service in India in 1944.

In the north-west corner of the Lady Chapel is the old cope chest, still in use. Mr Cecil Hewett has identified it as dating from the thirteenth century. At present, a label says it belongs to a century later; but this was based solely on the fact that it was repaired in 1408–9.

### St Stephen's Chapel

Adjoining the cope chest is the screen dividing St Stephen's (the Mothers Union) chapel from the retroquire. This was designed by Sir Ninian Comper, and was described incorrectly by Pevsner as a bronze screen. In fact, it is wholly of wood, the spindly shafts being stained dark brown and polished, and scenes of the Nativity of Our Lord highly gilded and coloured. There is no doubt that the resulting effect is very pleasing, even if it leaves a sense of irritation at the wrong material being used. All the furniture in this chapel, including the banner, was designed by Comper, and paid for, by instalments, by the Mothers Union of the diocese.

### Corpus Christi Chapel

The screen of the next chapel, now usually known by its original name of Corpus Christi, though later called that of St John the Evangelist, is also something of a rarity, since it came from the cowstalls of Lubborn House, Baltonsborough, near Glastonbury, having been given to the cathedral by the Misses Whitehead in memory of their parents in 1927. By the addition of some new carving the east end of the screen was converted into a canopy for the tomb of John de Godelee, Dean 1306–33, in a position exactly corresponding to that of his bishop, Drokensford (d.1329), at the entrance to St Katherine's chapel on the south side.

The carved Ascension over the altar was formerly in the east cloister on the south side of the entrance to the Camery. It was re-positioned here by George Kibble in 1864. When George Kibble applied for a vacancy as tenor vicar choral in 1862 he was instructed by the Chapter 'to make some Statue as a specimen of his ability'. This is not a normal requirement of a tenor voice, but he had evidently listed among his qualifications that he was a fully qualified mason. I suspect that his specimen carving was the corbel over the south end of the pulpitum, not usually visible because of shadow, but clearly revealed when the organ was taken down for rebuilding in 1973. This corbel with its gently smiling lips bears so close a resemblance to the thirteenth-century smiling heads in the Chapter House of Christ Church Cathedral, Oxford, that whoever carved the Wells corbel must have been familiar with the Oxford heads. He died in Wells after a long illness in October 1871, at the age of 42. The colouring on the Ascension group was restored very delicately by Maurice Keevil in 1975.

On the north side of the altar is the tomb of Robert Creyghtone [I], Treasurer of Wells 1632–60, Chaplain to Charles II in exile, Dean 1660–70, Bishop 1670–2. His effigy, carved in alabaster, shows him wearing cope, mitre and alb—probably for the first time. He rests on a slab of Tournai marble.

Under the north window in a recess is the effigy, said to be of John Middleton, who was Chancellor of the cathedral for less than three weeks in 1337, when he was immediately followed by Simon de Bristol. One suspects that there is a simple explanation, such as that the bishop had forgotten—if he ever knew—that Simon had been promised the next vacancy, either by the previous bishop or the king, and Middleton readily gave up the appointment to save fuss. Middleton, who was the Bishop's Commissary, was still living in 1350.

In the north-west corner of this chapel under the carpet are all the surviving fourteenth-century floor-tiles in the cathedral. Others were later discovered in the course of the excavations in the Camery. Many of these tiles were until 1976 covered by the tomb of Gilbert Berkeley, Bishop 1560–81, which had been moved here from the north side of the High Altar in 1703 to make room for Bishop Kidder's tomb there. In 1976 Bishop Berkeley's tomb was moved again to a much more suitable position in the north quire aisle (see p. 147), in order to uncover the tiles and make more room for worshippers in the chapel.

The glass in the east window of this chapel was thoroughly cleaned and re-arranged with the addition of 'postage-stamp' panels of old glass from other parts of the cathedral, cleverly put together by Dennis King in 1984. The north window, very much in the style of Burne-Jones and William Morris, was designed by G P Hutchinson of James Powell & Co. in 1902 in memory of Douglas McLean, the brother of Mrs Jessie Head who has already been named as a generous donor to the cathedral. This chapel is reserved for private prayer. The Blessed Sacrament is reserved here for the benefit of the sick and dying.

### The North Quire Aisle

The tomb of Giso of Lorraine, Bishop 1060–88, is the last of the series of tombs of 'Saxon' bishops. He was also the last to be known as Bishop of Wells. The monument next to his has the alabaster effigy of Ralph of Shrewsbury, Bishop 1329–63, in whose time the quire extension was completed and the Palace moat dug. This tomb originally stood in the middle of the presbytery, but was moved, says Godwin, because it got in the way of the celebrants and 'lost his grates by the way'. When it was suggested that this effigy might be restored and re-coloured, a former dean said this would be a pity as it would conceal all the interesting eighteenth-century graffiti. On the floor near this tomb is the slab covering the burial place of Dr John Sellek, Archdeacon of Bath, who was one of two clergymen sent by Charles II to obtain the release of English sailors captured in the Mediterranean and enslaved by 'Turkish' pirates of Algiers. Within six months the enormous sum of £10,000 was subscribed by English clergy in 1662 to buy the sailors' release. On the day before Sellek and John Bargrave, canon of Canterbury, were due to depart from England they were refused permission to leave the country because they had no passports, and were forbidden to take such a large sum out of the country. That evening they put their case to the king, and permits and passports were issued the following morning. In Algiers, dressed in their clerical habits and wearing their hats, they had audience of the king of Algiers. The outcome was that they had to buy all the English slaves singly from each individual owner, and were able to redeem all 162 of them, but at the cost of the full £10,000.

> 'All the difficulties lay upon me', wrote Canon Bargrave, 'by reason that my brother commissioner [Sellek] had never binn beyond the seas, nor could speak a word of their language, and so understood not his danger until it was over.'

Mr Brown, the English consul, suffered for it afterwards. He was enslaved, then beaten to death. It is a pity we do not have Sellek's version of the affair.

The next tomb, beyond the pulpit steps, is that of Gilbert Berkeley, Bishop 1560–81, transferred here in 1976 from the north-west corner of Corpus Christi chapel. Round the top of the tomb the following inscription has (or had) the letters which are here printed in italics filled with orange wax. Treat the orange letters as Roman numerals and add them together. The result is 1581, the year of the bishop's death.

SP*I*R*ITV*S ER*V*PTO SAL*VV*S G*I*LBERTE NO*V*EM*B*RE CARCERE

| | |
|---|---|
| TR*I*ST*I*S *I*N HOC | EN ÆTHERE BARK*L*E CREPAT |
| PR*I*NC*I*P*I*O | |

A̅N̅: D̅A̅T ISTA SALVTIS,

which was translated by Philip Martin, Chancellor of Wells 1971–9, as follows:

Rescued from the body's prison in early November
After sad sojourn on earth, now, Gilbertus Berkeley,
In heaven thy spirit crieth aloud.
(These letters show the year of its release.)

The letters of the first words of the first two lines of the inscription in the middle of the slab, *VIXI* and *LVXI*, when treated as Roman numerals, add up to 83, written alongside in Arabic numerals, to give the bishop's age.

83   VIXI, VIDETIS PRÆMIVM,
      LVXI, REDVX QVI FASCIBVS
      PRO CAPTV AGENDO PRÆSVLIS
      SEPTEM PER ANNOS TRIPLICES,

which Philip Martin translated:

My life is finished: my reward you see;
My light put out: I, who for thrice seven years
In virtue of my talents held high dignity,
Am taken home.

The other two monuments in this aisle complete the series of Saxon bishops.

### Stained Glass in the North Quire Aisle

The eastern window (no. 5 from north transept) has a left-handed dragon-killer (St Michael) in the tracery, made from the same cartoon, reversed, as the equivalent light opposite in the south quire aisle.

The next window (4 from north transept) has in the central tracery light a Crucifixion with the feet nailed separately. This was the convention until the latter part of the thirteenth century. Then one foot was laid over the other, and both fixed with a single nail. This custom was followed fairly strictly until the very beginning of the sixteenth century, when it became optional. So this appears to be either a figure retained from earlier glazing from the old part of the building, or a sixteenth-century repair, which is unlikely. It is not an eighteenth- or nineteenth-century repair, because that was done subsequently with a late piece of yellow angel's wing. In the main lights are the arms of John Clerke, Bishop 1523–41; the See of Bath and Wells (modern style); and William Knight, Bishop 1541–7.

The third window has a fourteenth-century St John Baptist in the tracery; and below, the arms of Richard Woolman, Dean 1529–37; Tudor Royal Arms; William Knight, Bishop 1541–7. The Royal Arms were cleaned and re-ordered by Dennis King in 1983. At the same time he re-ordered the inscription at the bottom, adding the word 'DECAN': 'Richard Woleman, Dean of this Church, to God Best and Greatest, 1537.' Knight was Woolman's executor and residuary legatee. Knight's arms, under a Dean's cap, although he was never Dean, probably replace those of Thomas Cromwell, Dean from 1537, but beheaded in 1540.

The glazing of the next window, second from the transept, is historically interesting, but unsatisfactory as a coloured window, because it is so overcrowded. That was the fault of Dean Plumptre, who commissioned it to celebrate Ken's bicentenary in 1885. Plumptre himself wrote the two-volume biography of Ken. This window is almost entirely painted with enamels, as was inevitable with so many small scenes to be depicted. It was the work of the firm of Westlake and Barraud. On the death of Philip Westlake, the window was completed by his brother, N H J Westlake, author of the famous four-volume *History of Design in Painted Glass*, 1889–94.

### The Undercroft

In the north wall of the aisle is the door to the undercroft, which is not open to the public. It contains the sacristy and the vestry (and practice-room) of the vicars choral and choristers, as well as almost the only storage space that the cathedral

*Boss in the vault of the passage to the undercroft or sacristy, showing two human heads being nuzzled by weird beasts.*

affords. It was built as the treasury, being originally divided into three compartments by wooden partitions, one for vestments and the cope chest; another for the mass vessels; and the third for the under-treasurer who had to be there at all hours of day and night. Originally there was no access from the outside: the heavy bolts fastening the doors could only be withdrawn from inside. By the door there is a piscina with a dog gnawing a bone carved in the middle of the basin. The water ran away through a hole behind the dog's front leg.

In the latter part of the nineteenth century and up to 1913 the undercroft was used as a coke-store for the six (only four at first) great stoves for heating the cathedral.

The pillars round the sides of the interior still have water-holding bases, but the inner ring of pillars, presumably added after work was resumed in 1286, have later bases and peculiar mushroom or umbrella-type capitals, very similar to those in Skenfrith church on the Welsh border, and also to the capitals in the nave of Grosmont church, probably by the same hand as Skenfrith. In Grosmont these capitals are combined with water-holding bases. Similar capitals occur in some other churches of South Wales. The lower part of the walls, to an internal height of about eight feet (2.4 m), has diagonal tooling, above that the vertical tooling, but because of the deeply projecting buttresses outside it would be difficult to associate the lower part of this building with the period before 1209, as in the nave. It would more likely be dated about 1240. The passage leading to the undercroft has a tooth-ache head for a corbel in the entrance porch (but unlike the series in the transepts); and corbels consisting of heads alternately right-way-up and wrong-way-up. The roof-bosses of this passage, which is now used as the sacristy, are almost the only pictorial bosses, apart from foliage patterns, inside the cathedral. (There are some later pictorial bosses in the cloisters.)

## The East Aisle of the North Transept

On the first pillar is a carved corbel deeply undercut in the manner of the capitals in the western part of the nave. It is in the form of a lizard or salamander eating currants. This corbel was copied on one of the embroidered wool stall-backs in the quire, with the inscription: 'Jocelyn placed me among the servants of the church.' The lower part of the triple shafts was cut off, and this corbel inserted to support the upper part of the shafts, c.1230–40, in order to leave a wide enough passage past the screens separating the former chapels in the east aisle of the north transept, to give easy access, firstly to the vestry built outside the north wall, and then to the steps leading to the Chapter House. The screens dividing these chapels were later replaced by altar-tombs, of which the tops are still visible as floor-slabs. These tops fitted into slots in the shafts in the east wall of the transept aisle. The tombs with their tops were lowered so as to be flush with the paving, c.1850, as part of the Victorians' tidying-up operation. The unworn portion at the head of these lias slabs shows where they were slotted into the wall-shafts; and the stone infilling of those slots is clearly visible.

The more southerly chapel, where the tomb of John Still, Bishop 1593–1608, is now, was dedicated to Corpus Christi or St David. Bishop Still's tomb was formerly on the south side of the High Altar. The northern chapel, where Kidder's tomb is now, was dedicated to Holy Cross. The tomb of Richard Kidder, Bishop 1691–1703, was formerly on the north side of the High Altar, displacing Bishop Berkeley. Later the Kidder monument was for a short time in St Stephen's chapel. The long epitaph below is largely devoted to a panegyric of Bishop Ken.

There were three Holy Cross chapels inside the cathedral, each presumably containing a supposed fragment or splinter of the cross on which Jesus was crucified: this one, the Bubwith chantry, and the chapel under the north-west tower, formerly used as the consistory court and one-time choristers' vestry. There was another Holy Cross chapel adjoining the east cloister, of which the foundations and Perpendicular west window tracery are visible to the north of the foundations of Stillington's chapel in the Camery.

The tomb against the north wall of the north transept is that of Thomas Cornish, who was titular bishop of Tenos (in the Aegean archipelago) 1486–1513, acting as Bishop suffragan of Bath and Wells in the episcopates of Stillington, Fox, King and Hadrian. At the same time, he was canon residentiary and first Chancellor, then Precentor of the cathedral, Prior of St John's Hospital, Wells, Vicar of St Cuthbert's, Wells, and other parishes, and Provost of Oriel College, Oxford. How did he occupy his spare time? When the tomb was placed here, the chapel of Holy Cross was still in use. The tomb seems to have been used as an Easter Sepulchre, and is now once again so used. All this explains why the north door, which originally provided entry to the vestry, without interfering with the altar of the chapel, now seems to be so very much in a corner when viewed from the Chapter House steps.

## The Chapter House

The stairs leading to the Chapter House are an impressive sight at any time, but the best time to see them is on a summer's evening when the declining sun pours its golden light through the large windows on the steps, while the passage from the north transept is deep in shadow. On the right hand wall of the staircase as you go up the diagonal tooling of the stonework is clearly visible to a height of about five feet (1.5 m), and above that the vertical marks of drag or comb take over. This is proof that an upstairs Chapter House was planned from the start, the lower part of the staircase being built at the same time as the undercroft alongside. Money obviously ran out not long after work had begun. We know that this happened soon after Bishop Jocelyn's death in 1242, when legislation in Rome over the issue of Wells *vis-à-vis* Bath proved so expensive, and

necessitated resorting to the Florentine money-lenders in Cheapside, London, whom Henry III himself patronized.

On the bottom walls of the staircase the water-table of the vestry built between two buttresses is clearly visible, with above it the blocked window originally lighting the transept aisle. Corbels depicting two canons or other clerics support the vaulting-shafts. Each of them nonchalantly kills a dragon or serpent with a walking-stick in his left hand. On the left, under the windows, are seats with foot-rests looking like double steps, on which sat the witnesses waiting to be summoned to give evidence in trials of presumed offenders on the cathedral staff. There were wooden doors, fixed in a wooden frame-work, in the small vestibule of the Chapter House, which prevented the proceedings inside from being heard outside.

High up on the east wall is the barred opening of a small room, which is approached by the separate staircase leading from the undercroft-passage to the Chapter House roof. This small room has been thought to be an anchorite's cell. But no mention exists in any of the Chapter records of the presence of any cell or anchorite in the cathedral at any time. The room is unfloored, consisting of a considerable depth of stone-dust on top of rubble filling. It would seem to have been just a space left between the stair-turret and the Chapter House vestibule, to which the builders gave ventilation and a door in case this space should ever be required for any purpose, such as storage.

When we reach the vestibule leading into the Chapter House, it may be noticed (but more probably will not) that this space is in the form of a rhomboid, not a rectangle. This is more apparent when one leaves the Chapter House, because the two delicate stone doorways with cusped heads to the arches and cusped spherical triangles above are not in line with one another. The front one does not obliterate its brother behind, but to anyone making a straight exit, the cusped heads overlap giving the impression almost of a woven crown of thorns. It may be that this was the master mason's original intention, but it seems more likely that it was dictated by the bay-system of the staircase. When the staircase was first begun, lancet windows were the normal manner of lighting, and a

*OPPOSITE: The steps leading to the Chapter House on the right, and straight on to the Chain Bridge and Vicars' Hall. Begun c.1240, but mainly built from 1286, and the upper flight 1459–60. On the left are the seats for witnesses awaiting their summons to the Chapter House, when clerical offenders were on trial.*

bay-design based on perhaps three or even four lancets was considered. The first bay, equivalent to the present half-bay at the bottom, was blind, being set between the buttresses of the original main building. Then three or four more bays, perhaps of the same width as the bottom half-bay, would have brought the entrance immediately in the centre of the west side of the octagon, already built (downstairs) to an internal height of about 8 feet (2.4 m) external 5 feet (1.5 m). But between the time when work was abandoned in the 1240s and its resumption in 1286 ('completing the new building begun long since'), wide windows in the Decorated style became fashionable. So the space to be occupied by the staircase was divided into two wide bays instead of three or four narrow ones. The result was that the second bay was no longer exactly opposite the centre of the west wall of the octagon. But the difference was so small that the master was able to make a virtue out of it.

Dr Richard K Morris has shown that the master responsible for the staircase windows was the designer of the Bishop's chapel, c.1280. The same moulds or templates were used for the mullions of the windows of both.

What now looks like a pierced screen at the top of the first flight of steps was then a window of the same design as the west windows of the staircase. The wall below was pierced and a doorway in Perpendicular style inserted when the staircase was extended and the Chain Gate and bridge built in 1459–60. The glass in the tracery lights of those lower staircase windows is the oldest in the cathedral, and must date from c.1290. The roundel at the apex of the upper window is a modern replacement of 1968, when the original roundel was taken out and cleaned by the Victoria & Albert Museum by ultrasonic vibration. It is now mounted and displayed on the Chain Bridge.

There was a change of designer for the Chapter House itself. The windows have a strong resemblance to the east and west windows of St Etheldreda's, Ely Place, EC1, the chapel of the Bishop of Ely's town house, built by William of Louth, Bishop of Ely 1290–8, and probably, on the strength of its resemblance to St Stephen's, Westminster, designed by Michael of Canterbury.

Is it mere coincidence that the glazier of the lower windows

*OPPOSITE: The vestibule or entrance to the Chapter House. Formerly there were wooden doors here, set in a wooden frame.*

of St Stephen's was a Wells man, sent back to Wells in 1294 to get more glass for St Stephen's? This order was cancelled in January 1296 on grounds of economy by John Drokensford, Edward I's Keeper of the Wardrobe, later Bishop of Bath and Wells, 1309–29. The main lights of the Wells Chapter House, said to illustrate the 'history of the Bible', but more probably scenes from *Genesis* only, were much admired by two independent visitors in 1634 and 1635, and it seems possible that when the glazier was left with some of the glass destined for Westminster on his hands in 1296, he sold it to the Dean and Chapter for their Chapter House, then nearing completion. This would be all the more likely if Michael of Canterbury, master mason of St Stephen's, Westminster, and also probably of St Etheldreda's, were also in charge of the Wells Chapter House. Whoever the master mason was, he was certainly in the forefront of architectural design at the time, not only in respect of the window tracery, the entrance arches already noticed, but also the extravagant use of ball-flower, possibly for the first time.

Some of the original glazing, without silver-stain, remains in the tracery lights, including Resurrection scenes in the topmost roundels, but the main lights were all smashed under the Commonwealth. Fifteenth-century coats of arms, brought from elsewhere, have been inserted in the east and west windows: in the east window, France and England quarterly (right), and (left) the same with a label of three points ermine for John of Gaunt. The west window has (left) Mortimer, and (right) the star and crescent badge of the Lancastrians, surrounded by the collar of SS. The first three of these were recorded in the east clerestory of the south transept in 1686.

The Chapter House seems to have been completed before January 1307. As a result of the dispute between bishop and Chapter in 1319–21, the bishop was no longer entitled to appear in the Chapter House except at episcopal Visitations. As he was not allowed to hold a Visitation of the Cathedral without the consent of the Dean and Chapter, this stall was not often occupied. It seems to have been repainted at some time not recorded. The arms, unfortunately repainted, of James I are in front of the east window over the bishop's stall.

The small head-stops of the stalls are said to be portraits. Almost certainly the carvers working at their bench in the lodge often had their eyes on the faces of the men working opposite, but in the literal sense we never had four popes and eleven bishops all at once, or numerous kings. There are seven men wearing coifs, legal dress (to keep fleas out of their ears), and worn by serjeants-at-law in particular, before the introduction of wigs as legal attire in Charles II's reign. The two heads on each side of a corner-shaft are here always humorous; two evidently so scurrilous that they had to be destroyed. The Archdeacon of Bath's stall coincides with the south-east corner, so his headstop wearing a coif, instead of having the strings tied neatly under his chin, is chewing them in his mouth.

The seat of Purbeck marble round the central column is said to be where witnesses sat after they had been heard, so that they should not mix with those still outside waiting to be summoned.

The prebendaries sat on the upper row of seats, each in his own stall, while their vicars sat on the prebendaries' toes on the bench below, thus providing a primitive form of heating. The spandrels of the canopies over the stalls have been covered with whitewash at some time. One guesses that Wells, being unable to afford the sculptured scenes of Salisbury, might have had painted pictures instead. Removal of the whitewash may reveal these once more. The complete restoration of the Chapter House from top to bottom is soon to be undertaken at the charges of the Friends of Wells Cathedral, one bay annually until the job is done.

Finally, there is the effervescence of the tierceron vault of thirty-two ribs to admire, for which no words are necessary.

The stairs continue upwards in a straight line, but narrower, and the passage then turns slightly at the top, so as to cross the road at right angles. This all adds to their fascination. We are then on the Chain Bridge crossing what was the main road used by London stage-coaches going to Exeter via Bath, which, having got up speed coming down St Thomas Street— then known as East Wells,—dashed under the bridge at 10 mph before changing horses at the Swan Inn. It continued as the main route into the city from the east, with petrol tankers, which just fitted through the arch, and other lorries shooting the bridge at 30 mph or more, right up to 1965, when Brown's Gate at the far end of Cathedral Green was closed to traffic.

## The Chain Gate

Permission for the building of the Chain Gate at Bishop Bekynton's expense was granted by the Dean and Chapter on 19 March 1459. The vicars recorded their thanks to the bishop

*'The effervescence of the Chapter House vault.'*

on the completion of the bridge on 5 February 1459/60 (see pp. 66–8). When completed, the passage entered the Vicars' Hall through the north wall, straight ahead. But this brought the vicars into the buttery, where the beer was kept. This was obviously unsatisfactory to some (especially the steward), so that way was blocked and a dog-leg entry made into Vicars' Hall east of the screens. This addition had the arms of Bekynton, not of his executors (as wrongly stated elsewhere), showing that it was completed before Bekynton's death in January 1464/5. The design of the tracery lights of the Chain Gate windows occurs nowhere else except in the porch of the Rib, which is the house next to the east of the Chapter House.

It is possible to get a glimpse through the new wrought-iron gates of part of the Vicars' Hall, but this will be described in its entirety in the next chapter (see pp. 165 ff. below).

The Chain Bridge now houses a small museum display compiled by Dr Warwick Rodwell of specimens dug up or associated with his excavations in the Camery in 1978–80.

# Chapter Four

# SURROUNDING
# ECCLESIASTICAL
# BUILDINGS

ANY GREAT WORK of art requires a worthy frame. The buildings surrounding Wells Cathedral could hardly be improved on. Let us start with the Bishop's Palace, since it is there at the wells in the bishop's garden that the story of Wells began. These three springs, producing more than 40 million gallons of water a day, afford a favourite view of the cathedral reflected in their still waters; but they are only accessible on those days when the gardens are opened to the public—normally Thursdays and Sundays in the summer, and on certain other days in aid of some special charity.

The present Palace was begun by Bishop Jocelyn in the 1230s. The only firm date we have is Henry III's gift of thirty oaks for building the palace on 2 August 1233. That is the part now known as the 'Centre Block', consisting largely of the Henderson Rooms, now used for conferences, meetings, concerts and other functions. The chapel was added by Robert Burnell, Bishop 1275–92, and the Banqueting Hall soon after. This was stripped of its lead for Edward VI's Treasury in 1552, at the same time as the Stillington Chapel (see pp. 23, 77—8 above). In Bishop Law's time, 1824–45, the east and south walls of that Hall were demolished 'to make a more picturesque ruin'.

When Richard Bagot was bishop, 1845–54, the hall occupying the centre block was divided into three reception rooms, and an upper storey was added by Benjamin Ferrey very

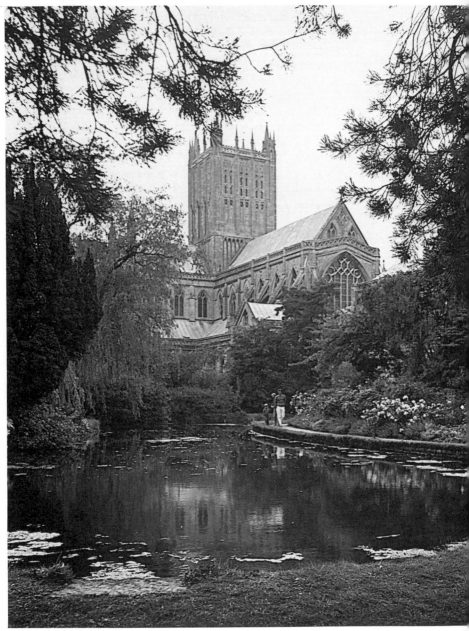

*The wells, which give the cathedral and city their name, are in the bishop's private garden, which is, however, open to the public on Sunday and Thursday afternoons in summer; and on certain other days in aid of charity.*

inconspicuously. He provided the present buttresses which he claimed were mere replacements of what had been there before. And he replaced the centre porch. The original porch was one bay to the north. A centre porch, looking like the work of Edward Blore, had taken its place by the time of Buckler's drawing in 1824. But Bishop Bagot would not allow Ferrey to do anything inside the building, where all panelling and carving of walls, doors and doorways consists of panels of plaster moulding bought by the yard. All this and the more successful ribbed ceilings were the work of 'an upholsterer of Bath'. As there were fifty-two upholsterers in Bath in 1842, it is impossible to name the culprit. The rather ugly windows are original, or, in some cases, exact copies by Ferrey.

The north wing, built for the kitchens by Bishop Bekynton, is now occupied by the bishop and his family. Bekynton connected that wing by a cloister extending in front of the chapel to the Banqueting Hall. The moat and wall were made by Ralph of Shrewsbury, Bishop 1329–63, who was granted licence to crenellate in 1340. From the evidence available elsewhere at this period it is apparent that the moat represented merely a status symbol, and had no defensive or offensive purpose. It would have been compatible with Ralph's nature for him to have planned it as an unemployment relief scheme in those unfortunate times, but it is extremely unlikely that the idea would have occurred to anyone in that era, however brilliant and however charitable.

From the walk along the south rampart inside the garden one can get a good view of Glastonbury Tor, of Park Woods and of the path across Palace Fields towards Dulcote, and the main road A371 running past Tor Woods (National Trust). The original road from Frome and Shepton Mallet followed the route of the present path. But when King John complained that it bisected the bishop's park and spoilt his hunting, he readily gave permission in 1207 for the bishop to have the road moved to the side of Tor Woods, where it runs today.

The masons bringing stone from Doulting for the building of the cathedral continued to have permission to follow the route of the path, so as to avoid the comparatively steep Constitution Hill of the 'new' road. So they were still able to have a downhill run almost all the way from Doulting to Wells via Dinder. This was made clear in Bishop Stafford's charter of 1433 permitting the masons to have a new entry from the Bishop's Green to their yard in the Camery, as well as

*ABOVE LEFT: Penniless Porch, where beggars sat for alms, built by Bishop Bekynton, leads from the market-place to the cathedral.*
*ABOVE RIGHT: The 'Bishop's Eye' gatehouse from the market-place to the Palace, also built by Bishop Bekynton, c.1451, for 200 marks.*

entry across the park from Doulting, and across his park from Keward, near the present Cow & Gate factory, when bringing blue lias from Street or Keinton Mandeville, or tufa from Ford Farm on the Poldens for the vaults of the Chapter House, Lady Chapel and retroquire.

The gatehouse from the market-place, known as the Bishop's Eye, was built by Bishop Bekynton at a cost of over 200 marks (£133. 6s. 8d.). The next gatehouse, known as Penniless Porch, which leads to the churchyard (Cathedral Green) and the cathedral, was very much smaller, but William Worcestre could not ascertain its cost. It adjoins the twelve houses, still known as the New Works, built by Bekynton, c.1453, and described by William Worcestre in 1480 as follows:

'This building is 100 paces long and cost about £500. Its frontage to the street is 80 yards or 152 paces.
N.B. There are 12 baywyndows in the space of 80 yards.

*The north side of the Old Deanery, showing the rooms occupied by Henry VII on one of his visits.*

In the elevation of three storyes of baywyndowes there are 7 lights in each baywyndow, making 21 lyghtes. And each of the said 12 baywyndowes is embatelled, viz. 3 embataylles in each of the 12 windows of le baywyndows.'

There were also three houses in Sadler Street, belonging to the New Works, two of them on the south side of Brown's Gate, and one on the north. The name 'Dean's Eye' seems to date from the second half of the nineteenth century. It is called Brown's Gate after Richard Brown, a shoemaker, who held the lease of the house next to the gateway on the south in 1553. This building, including the three houses attached, cost 200 marks (£133. 6s. 8d.).

The Old Deanery, the large building on the north side of Cathedral Green, was sold to the Diocesan Office by Christopher Woodforde, Dean 1959–62. The Diocesan officials are having great difficulty in financing the necessary repairs and maintenance, and discussions are at present going on to decide the fate of the Old Deanery and the destiny of the Diocesan Office.

There certainly was a Deanery in the thirteenth century. The present buttresses on the south face are clearly enlargements of much smaller buttresses. The visible parts of the building are of the fifteenth century, and the south front had two-light windows on the ground floor to light the storerooms and four-light windows under square labels on the first floor where all the main rooms are.

The most elaborate rooms are the Hall on the first floor on the north side, built or rebuilt by John Gunthorpe, Dean 1472–98, and occupied by Henry VII on one of his visits. Later deans have converted it into a chapel, but it is now the Bradfield Room, a most attractive committee room, used for meetings of all kinds, restored and equipped in memory of William Bradfield, Bishop 1946–60. The upstairs front room, panelled under Ralph Bathurst, Dean 1670–1704, and also President of Trinity College, Oxford, provides the main committee room. This panelling and the windows of the same room which face on to the Cathedral Green are said to have been designed by Sir Christopher Wren. But there is no evidence for this: they could be by anybody who by that time was experienced in that style.

Further to the east is the present Wells Museum, much of which is old. It seems to have been the house of the Chancellor of the Cathedral, though others, not Chancellors, also seem to have lived there; but Chancellors predominated.

Next is the much more elaborate house of the Archdeacon of Wells. This again is a much older house, rebuilt by Andrew Holes, Archdeacon of Wells 1450–70. The Archdeacons seem to have hung on to it until the famous Polydore Virgil had to surrender it to the Duke of Somerset in Edward VI's reign. Since then it has had an odd life, and was for many years a brewery. In 1886 it was extensively restored by Edmund Buckle, the cathedral architect, who claimed to have found evidence of old foundations for his stair-turret and large bay-window. It was then used for nearly ninety years as the very pleasant library of the Wells Theological College. When the College was transferred to Salisbury in 1971, the building was bought by Wells Cathedral School for its specialist music department. Agreeable noises issue from it at most hours of the day.

*Vicars' Hall, completed 1348, the Dining Hall of the vicars choral. This very pleasant room is used for small concerts and recitals, and for occasional meetings.*

### The Vicars' Hall

We now come to the Chain Gate, Vicars' Hall and Vicars' Close. First, we probably note a delicate little oriel window projecting to the west from the first building we come to. The western half of this building was an addition by John Henry Parker of Oxford to the existing kitchen of Vicars' Hall. The oriel window was a copy made by him of the one facing south just beyond the entrance to Vicars' Close. Also incorporated by Parker in his new building of *c.*1862 is the Norman dog-tooth stone, near the pavement. The bottom rooms of kitchen-block and Vicars' Hall are now occupied by the Freemasons of

Wells. But Parker, himself a Freemason, at first lived there himself, after getting William Burges to paint the walls and ceiling.

'The lower part of the walls were painted in imitation of curtains, which might not be strictly correct for the date of the building, but he could not afford silk curtains ... The walls, roof and arches were painted in lively colours, in accordance with high authorities on mediaeval decoration.'

The present Freemasons' temple was the store-room and cellar of the vicars choral, whose Hall and kitchen are on the floor above. The building erected at the charges of Bishop Ralph of Shrewsbury was completed and handed over at the end of 1348, when the Black Death in Somerset was at its worst. Edward III's licence in mortmain is dated 3 December 1348. The bishop's deed of gift of the building to the vicars choral was dated by him 30 December 1348, and endorsed by the Prior and Chapter of Bath on 1 January 1348/9, and by the Dean and Chapter of Wells on 3 January 1348/9. Already prior to that Alice Swansee, mother of one of the vicars choral who had died in office, had made her will on 7 November 1348, bequeathing to the vicars for use in their Hall

'one brass 32-gallon vessel; one better basin with a hanging ewer; and a table.'

This seems to show that the Hall was already in use. The plain wooden barrel-roof may have been intended as a temporary one, to be replaced with something more decorative as soon as the plague ended. Like most temporary buildings, it has not been replaced yet.

The Hall is approached by a straight staircase rising from Vicars' Close. The small circular staircase adjoining the main staircase on the west was merely to enable the cook or scullion to fetch more food from the store.

The original windows of the Hall, immediately to the east of the entrance have original stained glass in the tracery lights, St Margaret on the south and St Katherine on the north. The rere-arches are four-centred, which seems early for four-centred arches, until one remembers that Thomas of Witney, Joy's predecessor, had used them thirty years earlier on the pulpitum of Exeter Cathedral. The wave-mouldings at the side of the Vicars' Hall window-openings are typical of William

Joy's work. The same wave-mouldings are retained on the west side of the oriel windows next to the east, paid for by Richard Pomeroy, one of the vicars, who had been Keeper of the Fabric (i.e. clerk in charge of Fabric accounts) from 1488 to 1514. His portrait appears in one of the tracery lights.

Windows of William Joy's design remained in the whole length of the south side of the Hall until in 1459 Bishop Bekynton paid for the making of the Chain Gate and Bridge and steps down to meet the Chapter House steps, all at a cost of 500 marks (£333. 6s. 8d.). Then the Hall windows facing the Chain Bridge were removed, so as to give direct access on to the bridge. As previously described (p. 158) that brought 42 vicars twice nightly into the buttery where the beer was kept. So that wall was blocked and another entrance further east was constructed. Now with no windows in the western half of the Hall on the south side, the buttery and servants' passage were too dark. So the stonework of those two windows, which had been first taken out then blocked, was put together to make a single window of curious shape, high up on the west wall. This was not confirmed unil repairs in 1973 revealed that the centre mullion of that west window consisted of two half-mullions stuck together, which were the side durns of the previous two two-light windows. This centre mullion was then replaced with a new solid one.

Further east is the lectern, where no. 2 on duty (following the order of the vicars' houses) had to read the Bible to the assembled vicars during meal-times. They were not allowed to speak. It has been said that this lectern was given by Hugh Sugar, Treasurer of the Cathedral, on the grounds that it appears to have been built together with the fireplace, which has two initials carved in the spandrels under the mantel-shelf. These have been taken to be H S, for Hugh Sugar, but the first is undoubtedly a K and the second possibly L. There were very few Christian names beginning with K. But there was a Katherine Sugar, who in 1500–1 bequeathed 12 pence to the Cathedral Fabric fund. She might have been Hugh Sugar's sister or niece, and she might have given a new fireplace, and possibly a lectern, too. But this is wild speculation.

Over the fireplace hangs a picture giving the history of the vicars through the ages. Originally it hung at the foot of the great staircase on the end wall, facing the steps, and was seen by every vicar as he left and went to his home in the Close. There it suffered badly from the damp, and was moved into the Hall at the same time as it was repainted. In the middle of the picture at the top are the correct arms of the see (ancient). In the left upper corner is a bishop, somewhat brought up to date in the sixteenth century. Some say that this is Bekynton, and Ralph of Shrewsbury is in a lower layer of paint. He holds parchment or book on which is written (in Latin) the vicars' request:

'Disperst about the towne we humbly pray
Together, through thy bounty, dwell we may.'

To this the bishop replies:

'For your demaund deserts do plead, I will do what you crave.
To this purpose established here dwellings you shall have.'

The bulk of the picture is taken up with various vintages of vicars. Nearest to the bishop appear to be the most ancient, stretching back into the distance, all now apparently wearing London M.A. hoods; later vicars wearing collars have in many cases been given ruffs on top of their collars. Some at the bottom seem to favour neckerchiefs. The tomb-stone-like inscription at the bottom left was added after Elizabeth I granted the vicars their new Charter in 1592:

'What Ralph bequeathed in pious zeal
When we lived far and wide,
Good Bishop Bekynton increased
With grace and wealth beside.
Now in these days Elizabeth
Hath stablished us in all.
Good Queen, thy life be very long!
Thy sceptre never fall!'

It is obvious that the picture, or various parts of it, have been repainted or repaired many times. It was restored and reframed in 1862. In 1968 the Dean on behalf of the Friends of Wells Cathedral sent it for cleaning to the Victoria and Albert Museum. They returned it, saying that although there were many coats of paint, they were all so thin that it was unsafe to tamper with it.

The two wooden statues on the east wall seem to be contemporary with the building, and to have been made for their present position. Current thought suggests that they are

English. Malcolm Baker of the Victoria and Albert Museum wonders whether the wooden corbels supporting them belong to the statues. Although both statues and corbels are of oak, he had noticed that the corbels have at one time been worm-eaten, while the statues have not. That may have been just a case of seasoned wood being used for the statues, while for the corbels, initially being considered of less importance, green oak was used. While in the past they have been described as an Annunciation group, a Visitation group of the Virgin Mary visiting her cousin, Elizabeth, seems more likely. It is difficult to believe that the left-hand figure represents the angel Gabriel. Moreover, the figures on the right-hand corbel represent John the Baptist (Elizabeth's son) and Jesus, both wearing shorts and having a wrestling game. The little left-hand figures depict the Three Kings with their gifts of gold, incense and myrrh. The two large figures are very good examples of the curved body typical of the first half of the fourteenth century. The figures and particularly their heads are much elongated, because they are meant to be viewed from the high table of the refectory.

The panelling on the east wall is worth looking at closely, especially in the bay-windows, where small sphinxes and other Renaissance ornaments make their first appearance. In the centre is a run of linenfold panelling which first appeared in England in Henry VIII's reign. It was carved with a single stroke of a specially-shaped gouge, and was called 'drapery'. The benches in this room are definitely mediaeval, but cannot be dated precisely. The two tables are of the Restoration period. The bread-bin, to contain the bread-ration for 42 men, is almost certainly contemporary with the building, 1348. The sideboard was designed by J H Parker, c.1863.

Through the end door is the kitchen with its spit. The stone floor is supported by a stone vault below: all other floors are of wood. Near the centre of the room is an ordinary Somerset sink, carved out of a single block of stone, with a hole in one corner for the water to escape. Such sinks were still in use until recently in every farmhouse and cottage in the county. Here the water ran away along a channel cut in the floor which enables the water to leave the building by a small outside chute and fall on the heads of the unwary walking below.

In the first quarter of the fifteenth century further rooms were added over the main staircase. A small door and circular stair on the east side of the main door leads up to the Chequer, with its fine roof with inverted windbraces (in imitation of the

*The Chequer, c.1420, where the Receiver of the vicars choral took the rents for properties belonging to the vicars choral, which were supposed to cover their expenses and the maintenance of their buildings, but were never adequate.*

stone scissor-arches in the cathedral). There are other roofs of the same design in Wells, all apparently between 1420 and 1440. The oak shutters have kept out the wind and the rain for about five hundred years, since it was not until *c.*1912 that the windows were glazed. Till then the Receiver, elected annually from among the vicars, had to sit up here, warmed only by the fire, to receive payments of rent and other dues from tenants. Bishop Ralph of Shrewsbury, as well as giving the Hall, also endowed the vicars with an annuity of £10: £5 from the manor of Congresbury and £5 from the manor of Wookey. But this was hardly enough to maintain 42 men and their buildings. There were further endowments later, but they were never sufficient to keep the vicars' buildings in good order. This was one of the reasons why the Colleges of Vicars, here and elsewhere, were dissolved by Act of Parliament in 1933.

*The mediaeval filing cabinet, used mainly to hold the deeds of the vicars' properties. Each drawer has a slightly different shape, so that no drawer can be replaced in a wrong position.*

The fireplace where the Receiver warmed himself was enlarged *c.*1500 from the size of the herring-bone back to the ridiculous size, in proportion to the size of the room, of the present hearth. Think of bringing logs of that size up that staircase! Because of the joints with which the floor has been repaired in the middle (later than the joints at either end), it may be that a spark or hot ember, falling from the old hearth, has burnt away the middle section of the floor. (This floor is the ceiling of the main staircase.) When the floor was replaced, if our guess is right, the hearth was enlarged to its present size, but the fire remained no bigger than before, so that there should be sufficient area for sparks and embers to fall safely without causing damage.

The cupboard over the stairhead is where the Receiver could keep his pens and ink; and on the other side, the piscina is where he washed the ink off his fingers. There is a late seal-

*Cupboards, c.1420, to hold vestments and mass vessels, etc. in the vicars' Treasury in the tower below their muniment room. One lock has been cut away, and some doors are slightly warped; otherwise the cupboards are still in perfect condition.*

chest, dated 1633, which is useful for demonstrating the ledge on which a seal is kept, while the remainder of the chest was used to deposit books and documents.

The next room is known as the Muniment Room, being famous for its filing cabinet, c.1420, the beauty of which is that no drawer can be replaced in the wrong position. Each drawer was finished differently, the horizontal boards of oak being fixed over each row of drawers while the oak was still green, so that it assumed the varying shapes of the tops of the drawers. Then the next row was dealt with in the same way. The nail-heads, at one time thought to be arranged in a code, are seen to have been merely holding parchment labels in position, of which some fragments remain. These labels recorded the contents of each drawer: in most cases leases with the address of the properties leased. The north window is from Wynford's design and precise measurements of c.1395, which continued in use in the diocese for some years.

Down the narrow staircase built in the thickness of the wall is the Treasury, where the vicars' mass-vessels and vestments were kept, wholly separate from the Cathedral Treasury beneath the Chapter House. Here the Treasury door was fastened by a bolt operated from the floor above. The ten cupboards, apart from a little warping and the place where one lock has been sawn away, are as good as nearly six hundred years ago. The Treasury still has no glass in its window. The excellent state of all timber in the cathedral is due to the plentiful ventilation.

The Treasury and Muniment Room are in the tower. When this is examined from the outside in the Vicars' Close, it will be noticed that the present, larger tower is superimposed on an earlier, smaller one. It does not fit on the earlier buttresses. The stone vault under the tower is a later addition, evidently to prevent theft through the Treasury floor. In August 1443 Henry Martyn, one of the vicars choral, leased for life one tenement with two gardens in Monerys Lane (site of the Roman Catholic church in Chamberlain Street) for 6s. 8d. and repair of the same. In September 1448, Henry Martyn having died, the vicars resolved that his executors should make a vault beneath the tower adjoining the steps up to the Vicars' Hall at their own expense, instead of the repairs due to be made by him to the stable, etc. in Monerys Lane.

### Vicars' Close

The lay-out of Vicars' Close with gatehouse, hall, kitchen and store at one end; chapel, with library over, at the other end; and the vicars' quarters in between, built round a quadrangle, was the prototype of Oxford and Cambridge colleges built after this time. The quadrangle is one no longer. In about 1400

the vicars demanded gardens, and the front gardens were created and walled, leaving the central part of the quadrangle as a roadway. The whole rectangle looks long in proportion to its width: it is, but the effect is exaggerated because it is all built in false perspective, the space between the houses being nine feet (2.7 m) narrower at the top than at the bottom. Consequently it looks much longer.

The chapel is eight degrees out of square with the Close, because for the sake of economy its north wall was built on top of the wall of the Liberty. To conceal this deviation from anyone walking up the Close or looking out of the Hall window, the ridge of the chapel roof descends quite steeply to the west, the nearer side, so that from the Close or from the Hall, the ridge appears level, and the chapel at a casual glance appears square-on.

In his will, drawn up in 1363 three months before his death, Bishop Ralph referred to 'the houses which I have built for the Vicars'. In design they closely resemble buildings of William Wynford at New College and Winchester, but are in advance of buildings elsewhere. Moreover, the wall-plates in the vicars' houses, with their miniature machicolations closely resemble (as Pamela Tudor-Craig has noticed) the wall-plate in Hollar's print of the Great Hall in Windsor Castle (since destroyed), roofed by William Wintringham, 1362–5, probably under William Herland, when Wynford was master mason there. But Wynford was not appointed master mason at Wells until 1 February 1364/5, after Bishop Ralph's death. It is possible that he was in fact in charge here at that time, while a very old master was still alive, since appointments as master mason were usually for life. Wynford's own formal appointment for life, allocation of a house in Wells, and rate of payment consisting of a retainer of £2 a year for life, *plus* sixpence for every day he was present in Wells and engaged on the Fabric, would not be made until after the death of the old master. The only alternative explanation is that when the bishop said 'houses' he did not mean 'houses', but only the Vicars' Hall building. (*Domi, domos* seem to be often used in the plural form with a singular meaning, on the analogy of *aedes*. I do not know if this is just local usage.) Certain it is that the Close was virtually

OPPOSITE: *Vicars' Close, looking south. The Close tower, containing the vicars' Muniment Room and Treasury, covers the porch (vault 1448) leading to the main staircase up to the Hall.*

completed in its present form by 1382, when it is described as 'The New Close', a name which is kept in the Vicars' Act Books right up to 1905. This name may have been used earlier than 1382, but there is a paucity of documents relating to the vicars in that period.

The houses originally consisted of a single room upstairs and one down, each measuring 13 by 20 feet (3.9 × 6 m) internally. There was a latrine at the back under the stairs, and a small yard. No. 22 retains its original outward appearance. The heads of doorway and windows have been renewed, and the transoms of the windows, but most mullions appear to be original. (This house is occupied and not open to the public: the interior was very much adapted by J H Parker, c.1863.) Parker also restored nos. 26 and 27, which have the pheons (arrowheads) of his coat-of-arms on the modern label-stops of the windows.

Possibly the most striking feature of the Close is the high chimneys. These are not later additions in their entirety to the front of the houses, as previously supposed. Dr Rodwell has proved by excavation that the foundations of the chimneys are part of the original foundations of the houses. Courses of the front walls of the houses are not continuous on both sides of the chimney. On the chimneys are plaques bearing the arms of the see of Bath and Wells alternately with Bekynton's personal arms. Below them are the arms successively of the bishop's three executors: Hugh Sugar, Richard Swan and John Pope (or Talbot). Bekynton bequeathed the residue of his estate

> 'for some charitable purpose, such as the repair of roads and bridges or relief of the poor, or as my executors may see fit.'

The executors saw fit to give high chimneys for the poor vicars, and once again the poor old Somerset roads and bridges went by the board.

At Exeter in a so-called Obit Book (D&C 3675) is a record of the bequest dated 1401 by William Gerveys of a shop, the income from which was to pay for his obit. To this was added the sum of £12. 17s. 8d. contributed by the executors of John Burnebury, sometime canon and treasurer of Exeter, who died in 1459, to be used for the new building of eighteen chimneys in Kalendarhay, the Exeter equivalent of Vicars' Close. It is also apparent that the chimneys of the Bubwith Almshouse in Wells, on which work started in 1436, were subsequently extended upwards, much more simply, to which metal chimney-pots were also added, then or later, but recently removed. What was the reason for the raising of chimneys at this period? Was it because of a change to thatch or shingles as a roofing material? Or the increased use of coal (sea-coal), the extra heat from which was considered more dangerous to roof-timbers? Or was it that people were slow to realize that to provide efficient draught, chimneys built against a side wall must stand well proud of the ridge of the roof?

Originally there were twenty-two houses on the east, twenty on the west, one for each vicar. After Queen Elizabeth's statutes of 1592 fixing the minimum number of vicars at fourteen, and now that vicars were allowed to marry, each vicar was entitled to two houses. That left twelve single houses, as now. (There are fifteen double houses.) In 1663, to recover some of their losses during the Commonwealth, the vicars sought, and were granted, the permission of the bishop, as their visitor, to let out the twelve single houses to 'persons of good and honest reputation'. The present vicars choral (altos, tenors and basses of the Cathedral Choir) still occupy houses in the Close. Others are occupied by people working in the cathedral; a few, formerly held by the Theological College, are now filled with overspill from the Cathedral School.

The chapel at the top of the Close appears to be entirely of the fifteenth century. The earliest extant mention of it is dated 1447. It is remarkable that it should have been left unbuilt for so long; but at the same time one wonders why they required a chapel at all, when the vicars spent a good part of the day and night in the cathedral, as it was. The ends of the building are of random rubble, but the south face, facing down the Close, is built of an unusually fine, white bed of Chilcote conglomerate, such as is to be found in Ham Woods, Croscombe. Incorporated in it are some carved thirteenth-century spandrels, probably from the old cathedral cloisters. The arms carved on the door are those of (1) Hungerford. (His manor of Shipham was bought by Bishop Bekynton, who handed it over to the Dean and Chapter for the support of the vicars.) (2) The see of Bath and Wells. (3) John Stafford, Bishop 1425–43, subsequently Archbishop of Canterbury. (4) Nicholas Bubwith, Bishop 1407–24. Inside, the north wall is decorated with gesso work by Heywood Sumner, done towards the end of the nineteenth century, when the chapel was used regularly by the Theological College. Now the chapel and library room over are at the

disposal of the Chaplain of the Cathedral School.

The Chain Gate has already been mostly dealt with in chapters 2 and 3 (pp. 66 and 157–8). The question now is how the flat surfaces at the bases of the small arcades lining the footpaths on each side of the roadway have got so well-worn. Merely by sitting there day after day to see who went by, one could hardly wear it away so much or so regularly. Nor could it be done so thoroughly simply by fastening the chains across. In default of other explanation I suggest that the vicars' wives and the canons' servants from the Liberty used it daily for sharpening their knives, as one always did before the invention of stainless steel.

The next house, on the south side, known as The Rib (see p. 70 above) is especially interesting for its porch. The window has lights which are identical with those of the Chain Gate, otherwise unique. That gives us a date of c.1460. But under the window are three tournament-type shields which do not occur anywhere before c.1478, and first appear at Wells in the vault of the west cloister, c.1480, and on No. 14, Vicars' Close, the house immediately west of the Vicars' Chapel, where the four tournament-type shields bear the arms of 1. Bekynton; 2. College of Vicars Choral; 3. The See; 4. Stillington, Bishop 1465–91. On the shields on the porch of The Rib no arms can be deciphered. Tournament-type shields also appear on the southern bay-window built by Richard Pomeroy c.1510 over the Gateway to Vicars' Close.

Across the road from the Rib, behind a wall is the precentor's house, commonly called Tower House. It has often been suggested that this was the house of the master mason, who from the tower watched the building of the cathedral. But by the time the tower was built, Vicars' Hall would also have been built, and blocked the view in a south-westerly direction. William Wynford, the master mason, had his house, we know, in St Andrew Street, from 1365; the tower looks like his own work, and he might have climbed up the stairs there to watch work in progress in Vicars' Close. But it would probably have been just as quick for him to walk round at ground-level. In any case, in 1338 Tower House had been allocated as the precentor's house for all time. It seems to have been almost

OPPOSITE: *The windows of No. 14, which face down the Vicars' Close. The shields of arms are of the tournament type, like those on the porch of The Rib and on the oriel window over the entrance to the Close.*

always occupied by the precentor up until 1734; and then to have been treated as a normal canonical house. It is not clear how or when it became a Bishop's Rib, which it certainly was till recently. At the end of the nineteenth century it became the house of the Vice-Principal of the Theological College, and it was as a Vice-Principal's daughter that Elizabeth Goudge, the novelist, was born there. Later it became the residence of the Chapter Clerk; then of theological students. Since then it has been sold to a private occupier.

Most of the houses in Tor Street are older than they look. Opposite the last house on the left was the Torre Gate across the road, with a chapel over, which was demolished in 1445–6. The Gate itself is not mentioned after 1497–8.

At the city boundary on the Shepton Road (A471), where four small lanes meet, is wooded Tor Hill (National Trust). Here are the old quarries from which came the red triassic sandstone used in so many domestic buildings in Wells, such as the palace, the west wall of Vicars' Hall and the outer walls of the cloisters. From a seat halfway up Tor Hill, by following a left-hand path, can be seen the whole of the cathedral buildings in a frame of trees, popularly known as 'Cathedral View'.

At the bottom, a turn to the right following the city boundary, brings the visitor back to the Palace moat, and straight on to the Bishop's Barn, or, following the moat, back to the Bishop's Eye and the market-place, or to the cloisters and cathedral.

And that ends this short introduction to one of the most beautiful and interesting buildings, or sets of buildings, in Britain.

# BISHOPS OF WELLS

All Bishops buried at Wells unless otherwise stated.

| | | |
|---|---|---|
| Athelm | 909– 923 | *Canterbury* |
| Wulfhelm I | 923– 926 | *Canterbury* |
| Aelfeah | 926– 937 | |
| Wulfhelm II | 938– 955 | |
| Brithelm | 956– 974 | |
| Cyneward | 974– 975 | |
| Sigar | 975– 997 | |
| Aelfwine | 997– 999 | |

| | | |
|---|---|---|
| Lyfing | 999–1013 | *Canterbury* |
| Aethelwine | 1013–1023 | |
| Brihtwig *alias* | | |
| Merewit | 1024–1033 | *Glastonbury* |
| Duduc | 1033–1060 | |
| Giso | 1061–1088 | |

# BISHOPS OF BATH

| | | |
|---|---|---|
| John of Tours | | |
| (or de Villula) | 1088–1122 | *Bath* |
| Godfrey | 1123–1135 | *Bath* |
| Robert of | | |

| | | |
|---|---|---|
| Lewes | 1136–1166 | *Bath* |
| Reginald de | | |
| Bohun | | |
| (or Fitzjocelin) | 1174–1191 | *Bath* |

# BISHOPS OF BATH AND GLASTONBURY

| | | |
|---|---|---|
| Savaric | | |
| Fitzgeldewin | 1192–1205 | *Bath* |
| Jocelyn of Wells | | |

| | |
|---|---|
| (Bp of Bath & | |
| Glastonbury) | 1206–1219 |
| (of Bath only) | 1219–1242 |

# BISHOPS OF BATH AND WELLS

| | | | |
|---|---|---|---|
| Roger of | | | |
| Salisbury | 1244– | 47 | *Bath* |
| William | | | |
| Bytton I | 1248– | 64 | |
| Walter Giffard | 1265– | 66 | *York* |
| William | | | |
| Bytton II | 1267– | 74 | |
| Robert Burnell | 1275– | 92 | |
| William of | | | |
| March | 1293–1302 | | |
| Walter | | | |
| Haselshaw | 1302– | 08 | |
| John | | | |
| Drokensford | | | |
| (Droxford) | 1309– | 29 | |
| Ralph of | | | |
| Shrewsbury | 1329– | 63 | |
| John Barnet | 1363– | 66 | *Bishops Hatfield,* *Herts.* |

| | | | |
|---|---|---|---|
| John Harewell | 1367– | 86 | |
| Walter Skirlaw | 1386– | 88 | *Durham* |
| Ralph Erghum | 1388–1400 | | |
| Henry Bowet | 1401– | 07 | *York* |
| Nicholas | | | |
| Bubwith | 1407– | 24 | |
| John Stafford | 1425– | 43 | *Canterbury* |
| Thomas | | | |
| Bekynton | 1443– | 65 | |
| Robert | | | |
| Stillington | 1466– | 91 | |
| Richard Fox | 1492– | 94 | *Winchester* |
| Oliver King | 1495–1503 | | *St George's,* *Windsor* |
| Hadrian de | | | |
| Castello | 1504– | 18 | *(abroad)* |
| Thomas Wolsey | 1518– | 23 | *Leicester* |
| John Clerke | 1523– | 41 | *Minories, London* |
| William Knight | 1541– | 47 | |

William Barlow 1548– 53 *Chichester*
Gilbert Bourne 1554– 59 *Silverton, Devon*
Gilbert Berkeley 1560– 81
Thomas
  Godwyn 1584– 90 *Wokingham, Berks.*
John Still 1593–1608
James Montague 1608– 16 *Bath*
Arthur Lake 1616– 26
William Laud 1626– 28 *St John's Coll., Oxford*
Leonard Mawe 1628– 29 *Chiswick*
Walter Curll 1629– 32 *Soberton, Hants.*
William Piers 1632– 70 *Walthamstow, Essex*
Robert
  Creyghtone 1670– 72
Peter Mews 1673– 84 *Winchester*
Thomas Ken 1685– 91 *Frome, Somerset*
Richard Kidder 1691–1703
George Hooper 1703– 27
John Wynne 1727– 43 *Northrop, Flints.*
Edward Willes 1743– 73 *Westminster*
Charles Moss 1774–1802 *Grosvenor Chapel, W.1.*
Richard Beadon 1802– 24

George Henry
  Law 1824– 45
Richard Bagot 1845– 54 *Blithfield, Staffs.*
Robert John
  (Eden), Baron
  Auckland 1854– 69
Lord Arthur
  Charles
  Hervey 1869– 94
George
  Wyndham
  Kennion 1894–1921
St John Basil
  Wynne
  Willson 1921– 37
Francis
  Underhill 1937– 43
John William
  Charles Wand 1943– 45 *St Paul's, London*
Harold William
  Bradfield 1946– 60
Edward Barry
  Henderson 1960– 75
John Monier
  Bickersteth 1975–

# DEANS OF WELLS

| | |
|---|---|
| Ivo | c.1140–c.1164 |
| Richard of Spaxton | c.1164– 89 |
| Alexander | 1190–1213 |
| Leonius | 1213– 16 |
| Ralph of Lechlade | 1216– 19 |
| Peter of Chichester | 1219– 36 |
| William of Merton | 1236– 41 |
| John Saracenus | 1241– 53 |
| Giles of Bridport | 1254– 56 |
| Edward of Cnoll | 1256– 84 |
| Thomas Bytton | 1284– 92 |
| William Burnell | 1292– 95 |
| Walter Haselshaw | 1295–1302 |
| Henry Husee | 1302– 05 |
| John Godelee | 1305– 33 |
| Richard of Bury | 1333 |
| Wibert of Littleton | 1334– 35 |
| Walter of London | 1335– 49 |
| Thomas Fastolf | 1349– 50 |
| John of Carleton | 1350– 61 |
| Stephen Penpel | 1361– 79 |
| John Fordham | 1379– 81 |
| Thomas Thebaud of Sudbury | 1381– 96 |
| Henry Beaufort | 1397– 98 |
| Nicholas Slake | 1398–1401 |
| Thomas Tuttebury | 1401– 10 |
| Richard Courtenay | 1410– 13 |
| Thomas Karneka | 1413 |
| Walter Medeford | 1413– 23 |
| John Stafford | 1423– 24 |
| John Forest | 1425– 46 |
| Nicholas Carent | 1446– 67 |
| William Witham | 1467– 72 |
| John Gunthorpe | 1472– 98 |
| William Cosyn | 1498–1525 |
| Thomas Wynter | 1525– 29 |
| Richard Woleman | 1529– 37 |
| Thomas Cromwell* | 1537– 40 |
| William Fitzjames or Fitzwilliam | 1540– 47 |
| John Goodman | 1548– 50 |
| William Turner | 1551– 54 |
| John Goodman (restored) | 1554– 60 |
| William Turner (restored) | 1560– 68 |
| Robert Weston* | 1570– 73 |
| Valentine Dale* | 1574– 89 |
| John Herbert* | 1590–1602 |
| Benjamin Heydon | 1602– 07 |
| Richard Meredeth | 1607– 21 |
| Ralph Barlow | 1621– 31 |

| George Warburton | 1631– 41 | Edmund Goodenough | 1831– 45 |
| Walter Ralegh | 1642– 44 | Richard Jenkyns | 1845– 54 |
| Robert Creyghtone [I] | 1660– 70 | George Henry | |
| Ralph Bathurst | 1670–1704 | Sacheverell Johnson | 1854– 81 |
| William Grahme (after | | Edward Hayes Plumptre | 1881– 91 |
| 1709 Graham) | 1704– 13 | Thomas William | |
| Matthew Brailsford | 1713– 33 | Jex-Blake | 1891–1911 |
| Isaac Maddox | 1733– 36 | Joseph Armitage | |
| John Harris, Bp. of | | Robinson | 1911– 33 |
| Llandaff | 1736– 38 | Richard Henry Malden | 1933– 50 |
| Samuel Creswicke | 1729– 66 | Frederick Percival | |
| Lord Francis Seymour | 1766– 99 | Harton | 1951– 58 |
| George William Lukin | 1799–1812 | Christopher Woodforde | 1958– 62 |
| Hon. Henry Ryder, also | | Irven David Edwards | 1962– 73 |
| Bp. of Gloucester, | | Patrick Reynolds | |
| 1815–24; Bp. of | | Mitchell | 1973– |
| Lichfield & Coventry, | | | |
| 1824–36 | 1812– 31 | *a layman | |

# DIMENSIONS

Of the twenty-five old English cathedrals twelve are longer than Wells; twelve are shorter. Wells comes in the middle.

Modern English measurements were used when the cathedral was being built. So they are quoted throughout the book. The following tables will help with approximate conversion to decimal measurements.

| | | |
|---|---|---|
| Total length | 415 feet | 126.5 m |
| Width across transepts | 153 feet | 47.0 m |
| Width of Nave and Aisles, from stone bench to stone bench | 66 feet (1 chain) | 20.12 m |
| Width of West Front | 147 feet | 45.0 m |
| Height of Central Tower | 182 feet | 55.47 m |
| Height of Nave to Vaulting Rib | 66 feet (1 chain) | 20.12 m |
| Height of Quire | 73 feet | 22.25 m |
| Height of Western Towers | 124 feet | 37.80 m |

| | | | |
|---|---|---|---|
| 1 inch | = 2.54 cm | | |
| 12 inches | = 1 foot | = | 0.31 m |
| 3 feet | = 1 yard | = | 0.91 m |
| 5½ yards | = 1 rod, pole or perch | = | 5.03 m |
| 4 rods or poles | = 1 chain (i.e. 22 yards) = 20.12 m | | |

# MONEY TABLE

1 Farthing (usually written ¼d.) = one quarter of one (old) penny.

1d. (1 *denarius*) = one (old) penny.

12d. (12 pennies/pence) = 1s. (1 *solidus*) = one shilling: modern equivalent: 5p.

20s. (20 shillings) = £1 (*Libra*): One pound; or One sovereign.

6s.8d. = one-third of £1: known as 1 noble: modern equivalent: 33p.

13s.4d. = two-thirds of £1: known as 1 mark: modern equivalent: 67p.

Most large sums were described in the Middle Ages in *marks*, rather than *pounds* or *sovereigns*, although no *mark* coin ever existed.

One guinea = £1.1s.0d or 21s. At one time a gold coin, long obsolete; but fees and donations frequently continued to be paid in guineas after the coin had been discontinued.

# Acknowledgments

First of all, I must thank John Harvey for making me use my eyes, for answering my questions and for providing such a rich mine of knowledge. I must also thank all the other authors of the book *Wells Cathedral: a History*, edited by me in 1982; and especially Warwick Rodwell and Antonia Gransden for all the early history. In addition, I am grateful to Professor E L G Stones for giving me the reference to the vernacular comment on William of March's election as bishop; to Cecil Hewett, Richard K Morris and Jerry Sampson for miscellaneous information, and especially Bert Wheeler, the former Master Mason. I am also very grateful to the Wells Cathedral Guides and also to many of our visitors, for their stimulating questions; and to the Dean for his stimulating answers. All photographs are by George Hall with the exception of the following: Jonathan Robertson p. 53; Jerry Sampson p. 51. Line drawings are by Jane Elliot.

# Short Bibliography

Bilson, J: 'Notes on the Earlier Architectural History of Wells Cathedral', **Archaeological Journal**, 85 (1928), 23–68.

Bony, Jean: **The English Decorated Style**, Oxford, 1979.

Bowers, R, L S Colchester and A Crossland: **The Organs and Organists of Wells Cathedral**, Friends of Wells Cathedral, 7th ed., 1979.

Brakspear, H: 'A West Country School of Masons', **Archaeologia**, 81 (1931), 1–18.

**Calendar of Manuscripts of the Dean and Chapter of Wells**, Historical MSS. Commission, 2 vols. 1907, 1914.

Church, C M: **Chapters in the Early History of the Church of Wells**, Taunton, 1894.

Colchester, L S: **Stained Glass in Wells Cathedral**, Friends of Wells Cathedral, 6th ed., 1979.

— 'The Victorian Restoration of Wells Cathedral Church (Barnard MS)', **Transactions of the Ancient Monuments Society**, NS 4 (1956), 79–94.

— and others: **The West Front of Wells Cathedral**, Friends of Wells Cathedral, 7th ed., 1984.

— ed. **Wells Cathedral: a History**, Open Books, 1982, with chapters by Sir Robert Birley, R W Dunning, Antonia Gransden, David Greenhalgh,

John R Guy, John Harvey, Richard Marks, Warwick Rodwell, Pamela Tudor-Craig (Lady Wedgwood).

— and John Harvey: 'Wells Cathedral', **Archaeological Journal**, 131 (1974), 200–14.

Gardner, A: **Wells Capitals**, Friends of Wells Cathedral, 5th ed., 1975.

Geddes, Jane: 'Medieval Carpentry and Ironwork at Wells Cathedral', **Medieval Art and Architecture at Wells and Glastonbury**, British Archaeological Association Conference Transactions, IV, 1981, 46–51.

Harvey, John H: **English Mediaeval Architects: A Biographical Dictionary down to 1550**, 2nd ed., Gloucester, 1984.

— 'Wells and Early Gothic', **Report of the Friends of Wells Cathedral, 1978**, 19–24.

— and L S Colchester: 'Wells Cathedral: Architecture and Conservation', **Transactions of the Ancient Monuments Society**, 25, 1981, 104–12.

Hewett, Cecil: **English Historic Carpentry**, Chichester, 1980.

— 'The High Roofs of Wells Cathedral', **Report of the Friends of Wells Cathedral, 1972**, 12–15.

**'Historiola'**: A Brief History of the Bishoprick of Somerset from its Foundation to the year 1174' in

**Ecclesiastical Documents**, ed. Joseph Hunter, London, Camden Society, 1840. (This includes Giso's 'autobiography'.)

Hope, W H St John: 'On the first Cathedral Church of Wells and the site thereof', **Proceedings of the Somerset Archaeological Society**, 55, 1909, 85–96.

– and W R Lethaby: 'The Imagery and Sculpture on the West Front of Wells Cathedral', **Archaeologia**, 59 (i), 1904, 143–206.

Howgrave-Graham, R P: **The Wells Clock**, Friends of Wells Cathedral, 5th ed., 1978, reprinted 1983.

Lafond, Jean: 'La Résurrection d'un Maître d'Autrefois', **Precis analytique des Sciences Belles Lettres et Arts de Rouen pendant les annees 1940 et 1941**, Rouen, 1942.

– 'Le peintre-verrier Arnoult de Nimègue (Aert van Oort) et les Débuts de la Renaissance à Rouen et à Anvers', **Actes du XVIIIe Congres internationale d'Histoire de l'Art, Amsterdam 1952**, The Hague, 1955, 333–44.

Malden, R H: **The Story of Wells Cathedral**, London, 5th ed., 1955.

Reid, R D: **Wells Cathedral**, The Friends of Wells Cathedral, 2nd ed., 1973.

Robinson, J Armitage: **Somerset Historical Essays**, London, 1921.

– **The Saxon Bishops of Wells**, British Academy Supplemental Papers IV, London, n.d.

– 'Effigies of Saxon Bishops at Wells', **Archaeologia**, 65, 1914, 95–112.

– 'Fourteenth Century Glass at Wells', **Archaeologia**, 81, 1931, 85–118.

Rodwell, Warwick: **Wells Cathedral: Excavations and Discoveries**, Friends of Wells Cathedral, 2nd ed., 1980.

– 'Origins of Wells Cathedral', **Antiquity** 56, 1982, 15–18.

Singleton, Barrie: 'Proportions in the Design of the Early Gothic Cathedral at Wells', **Medieval Art and Architecture at Wells and Glastonbury**, British Archaeological Association Conference Transactions IV, 1981, 10–17.

Smith, J C D (photographs): **A Picture Book of Wells Misericords**, The Friends of Wells Cathedral 1975, reprinted 1983.

Wallis, F S and L S Colchester: **The Stones of Wells**, Wells Natural History and Archaeological Society, 2nd ed., n.d.

Woodforde, C: **Stained Glass in Somerset: 1250–1830**, London, 1946, and Bath, 1970.

Worcestre, William, ed. J H Harvey: **Itineraries**, Oxford, 1969.

# Glossary

ARCADE A row of arches supported by piers or columns.

ASHLAR Worked stone block with smooth face and square edges.

ASHLAR-PIECE Small vertical timber post, forming vertical support for lower end of rafter.

CANON A member of a Cathedral Chapter, responsible, with others, for the cathedral worship and administration. Canons are divided into (a) those who are resident or residentiary, with special duties, and (b) the non-residentiary or honorary canons, usually known as prebendaries in secular cathedrals, for whom it is now an honorific title only.

CHANTRY Endowment for saying of special mass at altar or chapel for the repose of the soul of dead person(s); a chapel built for this purpose.

CHAPTER A body of canons who, with the dean, are responsible for the management of a cathedral; derived from Latin *caput* = 'head'.

CLERESTORY The windowed top storey of a church.

CORBEL Projecting stone, sometimes carved, with a flat top to support further stone or woodwork.

CORBEL-TABLE A row of corbels set in the wall under eaves, to support the eaves or parapet, originally in imitation of rafter-ends, but now frequently merely a decorative feature.

CORNICE Moulded ledge projecting from wall.

CUSP Small, pointed projection in tracery of window or other opening.

DEAN The senior member of the Chapter, in charge of a cathedral and its worship.

DIOCESE The territorial area or see administered by a (diocesan) bishop. In the case of Bath and Wells corresponded almost exactly—and still does with minor adjustments—with the old county of Somerset.

DURN Door-post, or side-post of a window, whether stone or wooden.

EAVES The overhanging edge of a roof.

FACE-BEDDED Stone should normally be 'bedded' or laid in a building in the same direction as it lay in its normal strata in the ground. If it is stood with its grain running vertically instead of flat or horizontal, it is described as 'face-bedded', and is liable to quick decay.

FAN-VAULTING Vault consisting of a series of cones, half- or quarter-cones. All the ribs are equal, being radii of a circle.

HEAD-STOPS Carved heads terminating a hood-mould.

HOOD-MOULD Projecting moulding over an arch, either to throw-off water, or to give a 'finished' appearance to the arch.

KEEL MOULDING Moulding, otherwise round in section, brought to a point like the keel of a boat, on its outer edge.

LABEL A square or horizontal hood-mould.

LABEL-STOP Carved head, or other decoration, at the end of a label.

LIERNE Purely decorative ribs of a vault, serving no functional purpose.

LOUVRES Sloping boards (or slates) fixed in the openings of towers and bell-chambers to release the sound of bells, while keeping out the rain. In Somerset during the

Perpendicular period they were often replaced by upright stone slabs, with carved and decorative openings, known as 'Somerset tracery'.

MITRE JOINTS Joint in which the line of junction bisects the angle between the two pieces.

MOULDING Continuous decorative motif.

MULLION Vertical member dividing a window into separate lights.

OBIT Service of prayers for the dead; a requiem mass.

OGEE A reversed curve.

ORDERS Series of recessed mouldings or arches making up a moulded Gothic (or other) arch.

PISCINA A basin for washing Communion vessels; or simply for washing hands.

PREBENDARY A holder of a benefice (prebend) in a secular (i.e. non-monastic) cathedral, or cathedral of the Old Foundation. The title came to be used to distinguish a non-residentiary from a canon residentiary, though all are, in fact, prebendaries and all are canons. The prebend was an estate or manor which supplied their livelihood. But since the Church Commissioners took over all cathedral estates, the title has become merely honorific. To make things still more difficult, in cathedrals of the New Foundation (i.e. formerly monastic) the canons residentiary were called prebendaries, not canons. So Thomas Ken before his consecration was Prebendary of Winchester; Goodenough before becoming Dean of Wells was Prebendary of Westminster. This was rationalized in the middle of the nineteenth century.

PRESBYTERY The part of the chancel of a church between the quire and the altar.

PULPITUM Stone screen separating the quire from the nave. Often supports the organ. Sometimes called choir-screen.

QUARRY OR QUARREL (of glass) Small square or diamond-shaped piece of glass supported by lead strips, called calms, to make up a window.

QUIRE The old spelling, as in the *Book of Common Prayer*, which has remained in use ever since at Wells to signify the area in which the choir sings.

REREDOS Painted or carved screen behind and above an altar.

RESPOND A half-pillar or wall-shaft built into a wall to support one end of an arch or the springing of a vault.

RUBBLE Rough, unworked stone.

SET-OFFS A series of projecting, sloping surfaces as an architectural feature, together serving as weathering.

SHAFT A slender column, usually attached to a larger column or group of columns.

SOFFIT The underside of an arch.

SOLE-PIECE Small piece of timber lying flat on the wall-plate, and at right angles to it, so as to provide a firm seating for the ashlar-piece and lower end of rafter.

SPANDREL The roughly triangular space between the head of an arch and the extension of its vertical sides, or the space between the heads of two adjacent arches.

SPHERICAL TRIANGLES Triangles with curved sides.

STRAINER-ARCH An arch in compression to hold apart two pillars or walls, which would otherwise tend to lean inwards.

STRING-COURSE Continuous course of stone, usually in the form of a single roll, projecting from the surface of a wall.

SUFFRAGAN BISHOP An assistant bishop appointed to help a diocesan bishop. During the Middle Ages he took his title from an obscure Irish diocese or a remote part of the civilized world. By an Act of Henry VIiI in 1534, English suffragans were to take their titles from important towns in the diocese concerned. So the first suffragan bishop in the diocese of Bath and Wells was to be known as Bishop of Taunton. If an additional suffragan were appointed, he was to be Bishop of Bridgwater.

TIERCERON Additional decorative vaulting ribs springing from the corners of a bay.

TRANSOM The horizontal member of a window, linking the mullions and sides.

TRIFORIUM Middle passage of a cathedral or large church, formed originally by the aisle roof, with openings from the space so formed into the nave, quire or transept, nominally in groups of three. If this area has windows in its outside wall, it is known as a gallery or tribune.

TYMPANUM The head of a blind or partially blind arch or doorway, sometimes filled with carving.

VICAR CHORAL A prebendary's deputy who sang parts of the cathedral services on behalf of a canon or prebendary if he were unable to sing it himself, either because he was absent, or because he was incompetent. Vicars choral, certainly part of the cathedral foundation at Wells in the twelfth century, were in priest's, deacon's or minor (sub-deacon's) orders. Some were qualified to serve as chantry chaplains, others had various clerical or administrative duties. Now they are primarily professional singing-men as altos, tenors and basses in the choir, corresponding to lay clerks in cathedrals of the New Foundation. They earn their living by lay employment. Their cathedral engagement gives them a roof over their heads, and allows them to put jam on their bread.

VIRGER The rod-bearer appointed to keep order in a church, derived from Latin *virga*, a rod. So always spelt at Wells and several other places. Sometimes elsewhere spelt 'verger', from the French.

WALL-PLATE Timber member running longitudinally along the top of a wall to receive the lower end of rafters. These rafter-ends were often firmly attached to the wall-plate by means of ashlar-pieces and sole-pieces.

WALL-SHAFT See *Respond*.

WATER-HOLDING BASE This is merely a means of describing a moulding in use in the late twelfth and early thirteenth century up to about 1250, in which the mouldings of the base of a column are such that there is a horizontal hollow, so that if anyone should pour in any water, it would not immediately run away. There is no reason why anybody should.

WATER-TABLE Overlapping stone slabs so built into the end wall of a roof that they prevent rain from percolating through the joint where the roof meets the end wall.

WEATHERING A sloping surface, e.g. on top of a buttress or wall, to throw off rain, snow, etc.

# INDEX

**Bold numerals refer to illustrations or captions**